No Ordinary Man
By Kevin Browning

No Ordinary Man

Written by Kevin Browning

Editor – Tracey Fowler
Cover Design – Tracie Fry
Published in 2022 by KB Productions

Dedication

This book is dedicated to my beautiful children, grandchildren and their mothers. Also to all who supported me and even those who haven't! To everyone who served in the Falkland Islands in 1982 and to Argentina, as without you making the mistake of invading my birthplace in the first instance, I very much doubt I would have become as successful in life.

CONTENTS

Background

Introduction

Chapter 1 – Tough beginnings

Chapter 2 – An education

Chapter 3 – Making my way

Chapter 4 – Changes afoot

Chapter 5 - Captivity

Chapter 6 – Horrors of war

Chapter 7 – Bound for UK

Chapter 8 – Giving back

Chapter 9 – New beginnings

Chapter 10 – The world of tunnelling

Chapter 11 - Opportunities

Chapter 12 – Onwards and upwards

Chapter 13 – Moving on

Chapter 14 – Small world

Chapter 15 – GTE Doha

Chapter 16 – Everyone deserves a chance

Chapter 17 – Pushing for change

Chapter 18 - Proud

Chapter 19 - Support

Chapter 20 - Reflection

Background Information

The Falklands are a remote group of small islands in the South Atlantic, around 8,000 miles from the UK, made up of West and East Falkland plus many very small islands. In the 1960s and 70s the two main rugged islands were home to sheep farms and abundant birdlife with little access to the outside world. The locals, known as 'Kelpers,' due to the wealth of sea kelp on the shores, relied on radio for communication; there was no telephone network and no TV. Supplies to the island were limited. Tinned food, grain, alcohol and emergency supplies were shipped in sporadically. Alcohol arrived on the farms just a couple of times a year and was rationed to the locals, not only to ensure it lasted but also in an attempt to avoid drunkenness and any subsequent bad behavior or injuries. Every home baked its own bread and cakes, and most households owned a cow to provide them with milk. Hens provided eggs. The island inhabitants mostly lived off the land eating what they grew and the animals that were kept; meat was given free to all those who worked on the farms – mutton in summer, beef in winter.

No Ordinary Man

Introduction

I have spent many years doing what I consider to be my best to please, pacify and help others with whom I have had the pleasure and sometimes displeasure of becoming acquainted with on life's journey.

I worked out at a very early stage in life that if you are not able to change things for the better in the position you are in, if you're determined enough, you can work yourself into a role that will allow you to be heard and make those changes.

I believe in a need for accountability at all levels, but especially at senior level. If I was ever elected to public office, I would passionately pursue that accountability from all.

I have written this book partly to document my history and to share with those close to me, details of my past they may not have previously known. It is also my desire to demonstrate that success can be achieved by hard work, passion, vision and above all, determination. I know from experience it's very hard to stop a determined person. I hope my story shows you don't have to be governed by your past, no matter what you have had to endure and you don't need to be held back because you didn't receive the best academic education. I want you to see that life isn't always an easy ride for the majority of us, despite what you see on the outside; we all have our demons. You will see how I have made mistakes and taken hard knocks but each time I fell or was knocked down, I got back up. My wish is that this book might motivate people to not give up, to keep trying and to reach their goals, no matter what those goals are. Decide what you want from life; it doesn't have to be money or material things, but once you know what you want, go for it. Always look for solutions, not problems; be successful and be happy, whatever path you choose.

CHAPTER 1

Tough beginnings

I was born in September 1964 in Port Stanley, the capital of the Falkland Islands. We lived in a house 10 miles from anywhere on East Falkland, a house which at that time could only be reached on horseback, by Land Rover or on foot.

On Boxing Day 1964, when I was just three months old, my father sat in our modest home with two friends who had joined us to celebrate Christmas and were staying in a small caravan next to the house. As evening fell, my mother put my brother Gavin to bed and tucked me in to my cradle before retiring herself. Meanwhile the men drank the remains of the alcohol rations before turning in.

When my father awoke the next morning he reached for my mother but she wasn't there. He rose and went to look for her, shocked to the core to find her in the arms of one of his so called friends. Consumed with rage, my father grabbed his 303 Lee-Enfield rifle and held it to my young head screaming: "I'll shoot; this bastard isn't mine anyway is he?" A struggle ensued. Obviously at only few months old at the time, I have to rely on the accounts of others here, but the fact is I lived to tell the tale. My future step-father, Kelvin, escaped on a motorbike, narrowly dodging the bullet sent after him, while my mother grabbed what belongings she could. She gathered up Gavin and me and with the help of my uncle we escaped in a Land Rover and then a float plane and made it to my grandparents' home at Egg Harbour. My mother needed to find work to support her family so she moved to the capital, Port Stanley, also known as Stanley and of course now given city status by Her Majesty The Queen. My mother took Gavin with her, him being the older child, but left me with my grandparents and two aunts, knowing that working and looking after two small children would be an impossibility for her. She found work at the hospital in Stanley and continued her affair with Kelvin. I occasionally visited them in Stanley. One vivid memory is of a cousin pulling me up the steps outside the house by my tiny wrist and the excruciating pain I experienced as he did so. We later discovered the helping hand had resulted in a fractured wrist for me. My mother married Kelvin and they moved to a shepherd's house in Camp Verde. Despite having now forged a close relationship with one of my aunts, who I by now considered my mother, I was taken back from my grandparents' care at the age of four, to live as a family in 'the Verde' with my mother, Kelvin and Gavin. Kelvin would ride into the farm settlement once a month and return with food supplies that he'd bought in bulk to see us through. My eyes would light up as he unloaded the supplies into our store; there was so much food, which was a huge temptation for me at such a young age. One day Kelvin caught me dipping a spoon in to a 7lb tin of raspberry jam. He was absolutely furious that I dare do such a thing and ordered me to stay there, forcing me to keep eating until I was sick. I still don't eat raspberries to this day as a result.

Uncle Keith stayed with us at 'the Verde'. I got on well with Uncle Keith, well most of the time anyway and in later years I would go to stay for a few days here and there with him, his wife and his son, which would always be fun times. Keith had a Triumph 650 motorbike that fascinated me. I dreamt of riding off on this shiny powerful machine. Sometimes I would climb on to it as it stood against the fence and imagine I was on the open road. Uncle Keith would get mad if I so much as touched it and so after catching me sitting on his pride and joy for a second time I endured a few whacks on my backside. I felt indignant. Later while he slept, in retaliation, I crept under his bed and set fire to it. That also gave me a sore backside. I don't know what the fascination was with fire, but another time I managed to set fire to a large valley of dry grass which saw the whole farming community come out to contain it; another sore backside for me!

I wasn't always treated right as a child. Don't get me wrong, I can remember some fun and happy times, but for the majority of my childhood I feel life was anything but fun and happy. We had an old tame horse called Geeky at 'the Verde', which was used around the farm. One day Kelvin lifted me onto her back before placing a hot potato under her tail. She bolted, much to Kelvin's amusement. Unfortunately for me, my riding skills failed me and I felt lucky not to have been killed when I eventually fell off.

I definitely carried a feeling of worthlessness which created a desire to gain attention. I guess this is why I was so often mischievous as a child, naughty even. That got me attention, even if it was the wrong kind. Sometimes, after doing something wrong I would be locked in a dark shed for hours on end before being whipped with a horse whip as my punishment. Beatings, which had previously given me a sore backside, progressed to hard punches, below the head of course so that the bruising didn't show. There was no-one to tell, even if there was it would probably have resulted in more beatings, so I just accepted this was how it was.

After a couple of years we moved from 'the Verde' to Douglas Station where my mother took a cook's position at the bunkhouse. I think she had by now realised if we were to have money to feed and clothe us she would need to be the one bringing it home, as while Kelvin worked hard he drank harder. The drink brought out Kelvin's wicked side too, something I would often feel the need to tackle in order to protect my mother. Luckily my mother was an exceptionally strong woman. She often worked 15-hour days feeding many farm workers with limited ingredients and a bit of imagination, in addition to making the obligatory daily bread and cakes.

CHAPTER 2

An education

Another new chapter in my young life began at the age of six when I was sent off to school. A 40-bed boarding school, built in 1956, stood on the outskirts of Darwin, close to Goose Green and about 60 miles from Stanley. In a relatively isolated location, reachable only by means of a clay track, it was built with money provided by the Falkland Islands Company, although it was government equipped and maintained. The school's purpose was to facilitate the education of children born to the farm workers. It had a caretaker/handyman, whose wife was a matron/nurse, five teachers on contract from the UK and a headmaster. On the ground floor there were four classrooms, one infant, one junior and two seniors; the teachers lived above the kitchen and dining room, which doubled up as an assembly room. There were also four dormitories on the first floor, two senior and two junior, plus communal bathrooms.

Children from the farming community would be sent to the school at the age of seven, although I was somehow enrolled at the age of six when seven-year-old Gavin started at the school. I'm not sure how they pulled that off, but I guess the thought of having me about my parents' feet for another year motivated them to make it happen.

The boarding school, away from the main town, kept the farmers' children separate and the level of education we received was limited to ensure we didn't have aspirations 'above our station'. We were expected to look no further than farming for a living, carrying on the local tradition. The school offered little interest in us as individuals, there was certainly no encouragement, no real care and definitely no love. There was no such thing as privacy at the school either, as previously mentioned, even the bathrooms were communal. There was a rota for us all to have two baths a week, whether we needed them or not! And it was two in a bath at the same time to save on water.

Things were quite regimented, for example - we each had our own lockers in the changing rooms where we kept our PE kit and woe betide anyone who didn't keep their kit in order. I remember one evening we got called back to the changing room because some of the shoes hadn't been put away correctly. The result was each and every one of us in the group getting caned. It wasn't the only time I received the cane as a punishment for something I didn't do. Every day we had prep after supper, which was done in the classroom in silence. We had one rubber between the whole class; if you needed it you put your hand up and it was passed around the class to you. One particular evening I'd watched one of the girls bite the rubber in half. When it was returned to the teacher at the end of prep there was hell to pay. The teacher was furious and demanded to know who was responsible. When no-one owned up we were informed we would all sit there, all night if necessary, until the culprit did own up. With no-one actually accepting responsibility for the bitten rubber and watching the clock ticking away, I decided I would say I did it. I just couldn't see the point of us all sitting there all night, so I decided to take the rap; or the cane once again as it turned out to be! Word did eventually get out that I had not been the one to break the rubber, but it was too late to worry about it by then.

Outdoor pursuits were timetabled for Thursday afternoons. I was quite excited to find out what that would be but I should have known better. Outdoor pursuits amounted to a trek along the primitive road, which was no more than a clay track full of pot holes, which led to and from the school. Armed with wheelbarrows, we had to make our way to the beach, load pebbles and stones from the beach in to the wheelbarrows and were then tasked with filling the holes in the track. Our outdoor pursuits amounted to child labour, fixing the road!

Those with parents or relatives living close to the school were allowed to go home at weekends. My grandparents had by this time moved to Goose Green and so Gavin and I were allowed out for visits some weekends. My mother and stepfather had moved to San Carlos and travelled over to see us at the grandparents' house. Gavin seemed to have many more weekends 'home' than I ever did; I think they saw me as a bit of a handful and too much trouble to have at home too often. I remember vividly however, accompanying Gavin to the grandparents' house on the weekend of my seventh birthday. I was full of anticipation, reaching the ripe old age of seven and wondered what the day would hold. My birthday came and went and I was returned to school without anyone even remembering it was my birthday. The disappointment ran deep although I'm not sure why as there was plenty of it throughout my childhood.

I quite liked sports at school, however even that had its moments. Playing rounders one day, an over enthusiastic teacher caught me full whack in the face with the bat as he swung for the ball. It knocked me clean out cold and when I came round one half of my face was twice the size of the other half. I was sure my jaw or cheek bone was broken. No x-ray for me though, I was just told to go to my dorm. The staff hushed it up and the incident was never spoken of again. The teacher didn't do it on purpose, but surely I should have at least received some medical care and maybe an apology? Another sports memory for me was one day when playing football the teacher placed me in goal. A much bigger lad took a shot with the very heavy leather football. I gave it my all and managed to save the ball, but the kick had been made with such force that it actually broke my wrist. On this occasion things worked in my favour somewhat. The British naval ship HMS Chichester, I think, just happened to be patrolling close to the Falkland Islands and so they sent a helicopter to the school. They flew in, picked me up in the helicopter and flew me to the ship which was equipped with an experienced doctor and an accompanying medical team. On board, they put my wrist in a cast and I remember being spoilt rotten for, what felt like, the very first time in my life. They made such a fuss of me and fed me some of the most delicious food I'd ever tasted. With our diet at the school being extremely basic, the rich food I experienced was a bit of a shock for my stomach and as I returned to school I was rather ill.

There is no doubt in my mind that some of the teachers at the school were real bullies. One day in sports we had running. Gavin suffered from asthma but the teacher, despite Gavin already showing signs of an imminent asthma attack, insisted he continued to run in the wet and cold weather until he collapsed. He was taken to hospital and this was one of the occasions a red mist descended on me. I ran full pelt at the teacher, furious he had put my brother in danger like that. No-one was asked to answer for Gavin's hospitalisation; 'just one of those things' they said.

Outside of lessons we were allowed to borrow one of the fishing rods that hung in the headmaster's office to go fishing down at the creek. I really enjoyed doing that but one day I was walking through the school with the rod in my hand when one of the lads acting the twit started jumping around saying: "I'm a fish catch me." Well I did! I gestured as if I was fishing, casting the rod in his direction. Unfortunately for him, the hook on the end of the rod caught him right under his top lip. If he was the fish, he was my catch of the day but you can guess what happened next... yes, the cane again for me!

At break time one of the older and bigger boys would stand in the doorway leading outside and demand that we smaller kids punch him in the stomach to show how strong he was. When my turn came I punched him hard in the testicles. Once he'd recovered, when he found me I received a real beating, but he never stood in the doorway again.

Gavin and I went home to San Carlos for the school holidays, something we should have looked forward to but something I dreaded from the bottom of my heart. My step grandfather had moved in to the family home by this time. Perhaps he saw me as an easy target or maybe he thought he'd punish me for my childish antics and misbehavior, I don't know. I was just seven-years-old when the abuse started. It affected me deeply in a number of ways, one of which involved bed wetting. When I arrived back at school after the holidays, if I wet the bed the teacher would make me bath in cold water and would then send me, carrying my soiled sheets, to the washroom, making me pass through the dining room while the whole school were in there eating breakfast. It was humiliating and caused me huge embarrassment. I regularly met a young lady in the washroom who was also washing her sheets. I would hang her sheets outside on the line for her as to limit her shame and I would wonder if she, like me, was also encountering horrors that traumatised her.

A doctor visited the school on occasions. One morning at the end of assembly the headmaster asked if anyone wanted or needed to see the doctor, who was making a visit to the school that day. I had never discussed the abuse with anyone, it felt like a black cloud hanging over me, a heavy weight upon my shoulders, but maybe I could tell a doctor. Maybe he could help stop the bed wetting if nothing else. Drawing on every ounce of courage, I said I would like to see the doctor. I was asked why I needed to see him but was far too ashamed to give the real reason so I made up a stomach problem. I think the staff had a feeling I was making it up, but they obviously didn't know why. I was told I would be wasting the doctor's time, I wouldn't be seeing him, I just needed to get back to the classroom and that was that. It was the one time I had decided to tell someone about the abuse and after mustering up the courage, the opportunity was denied me. I never spoke of the shame again until I met my beautiful wife, Claire, many years later.

By 1976 my mother and Kelvin had moved to Goose Green. My mother got work as a cook at the boarding school and later worked as a cook in the bunk house at the farm. During the summer holidays, from the age of about 11 or 12, we kids would work in the sheep shearing sheds. It was extremely cheap labour but it kept us out of mischief and helped the farming world go round. The Falklands' economy depended heavily on wool production and export. The medium fine wool was highly sought after.

Goose Green had the second largest sheep shearing shed in the world. It would hold up to 6000 sheep all waiting to be shorn. At full strength 24 men would shear at one time. As children we were in awe of their speed and skill. We would carry wool, sweep up and fill the pens in front of the shearer. The shearers were very competitive. One time a local man laid a challenge against a New Zealand contractor who was the 'gun' (meaning the fastest shearer) at the time. By mid-afternoon it was clear the local was not going to catch up with him and I heard the 'gun' say to him as he collected his next sheep: "Out of the way shallow water, a deep-sea wave is rolling by." I was 12-years-old and had a hero!

CHAPTER 3

Making my way

I left school at the age of 14; 14½ to be exact, and went to work on the Falklands' Irish built service boat, A K Ilen. This allowed me to save for my first, very own, motorbike which allowed me to ride in to Stanley on a regular basis to make new friends of the female kind.

Sadly the job didn't last much more than a year. The skipper fired me when I refused to take the bike onboard ship for a journey. I insisted on riding the motorbike and meeting the boat when it docked. It turned out disobeying the skipper wasn't my best decision. I stuck with the motorbike and drove it to the jetty at Goose Green to meet the boat as it sailed in. I tied the boat up as it docked, just in time for the skipper to appear and fire me! By this time, with Gavin and I now 'all grown up', my mother had given Kelvin his marching orders and had started seeing the farm carpenter, who several years later she married (after divorcing Kelvin of course).

As the 1970s came to close I took a job as a shepherd, firstly in San Carlos and then at Goose Green, living alongside fellow shepherds and farm workers and sleeping in a bunk house on the farm at Goose Green, which as the largest farm on the Falklands, at that time had around 120,000 sheep. It would be quite normal for shepherds to travel 20 miles or so on horseback just to reach an area where the sheep needed to be gathered. We referred to the individual areas where the sheep were kept as camps, many of which covered up to 10 square miles. A group of shepherds would head out together in an extended line spanning a wide area. Each would go to different camps herding up the sheep to take the back to Goose Green to be shorn. Each shepherd would be expected to take care of anything up to 1,000 sheep each. Once we had rounded up the herd under our direction, we would head to a designated area to meet up. The next day we would drive up to 10,000 sheep back to the shearing shed and then a few days later we would return them, all sporting grade II haircuts (the sheep not the shepherds).

It was on one of these occasions I found myself in the middle of the extended line with my dog called Cap. Rain was running off my back, I was bored and was a picture of absolute misery. To break the boredom I decided I would visit the next in line and after riding about a mile I saw the next in the line was Sandy, a cantankerous old shepherd. As I approached him, I said: "I think the rain is going to stop." To which he replied, as he rode away from me: "It will be the first time ever if it doesn't!" This was the life that had been mapped out for me, as it was for the children of so many farm workers on the islands and it wasn't a bad life. It was hard physical work but that kept us fit and there was good camaraderie among the workers, well most of them anyway.

Every weekend my best friends Graham, Toogles and I would make the 60 mile trip to Stanley on our motorbikes to meet up with our girlfriends. The journey was almost all off road riding and could take up to four hours in winter. We'd always have plenty of fun but would make sure we were back at work in Goose Green by 6am on the Monday morning without fail.

I had grown up under the threat of Argentina, located around 300 miles off the Falklands, claiming my birthplace. British Navy Captain John Strong made the first recorded landing on the islands in1690 but in the years that followed sovereignty was often contended. In 1820 Argentina proclaimed sovereignty but by 1833 a British force had expelled any remaining Argentine officials and began a military occupation. In 1841, a British Lieutenant Governor was appointed and from then on, a British community of around 1,800 people worked hard to become as self-supporting as they could be and they were proud to be so. I remember very well when I was growing up, the adult conversations about whether Great Britain, or 'home' as we Kelpers called it, would always hold our homeland in its hands.

Life on the Falklands remained pretty much unchanged throughout most of the 20th century, despite persistent diplomatic efforts by Argentina to regain control of the islands... until 1982 that is.

In 1981 the British Foreign Minister arrived in the Falkland Islands to hear the voice of the islanders. We were asked to vote as to whether or not we should remain under the protectorate and government of Great Britain. The alternative to us seemed to be reverting to Argentine rule which no-one wanted. The minister left the islands in no doubt that we 100% wanted to remain British. It was official.

Meanwhile there was unrest in Argentina. The military junta in Argentina, led by Lieutenant General Leopoldo Galtieri, was reported to be responsible for the disappearance of up to 30,000 Argentine residents who had criticised the junta for its oppressive rule and the way it was managing the Argentine economy. Maybe in an attempt to regain favour and promote a patriotic feeling, or maybe just because he thought the Argentines could, in 1982 Galtieri planned an Argentine invasion of the Falklands, believing it was unlikely the British would retaliate. After all they were around 8,000 miles away. How wrong he was!

CHAPTER 4

Changes afoot

I continued to live and work as a shepherd at Goose Green and each evening, with no telephone service and no television on the islands, we would tune in to the radio to listen to the news that broadcast direct from Port Stanley. From time to time we would also tune into the BBC World Service to keep up with world affairs. A few Kelpers had VHF transmitters which enabled them to communicate worldwide via the Victor Papa 8 Falkland call sign. Little did they know how important this would soon become.

On 2nd April 1982 we were given word that the Governor of The Falklands would be speaking on the daily radio bulletin and as many islanders as possible should tune in. That evening as we sat in anticipation, the Governor announced an Argentine naval fleet had set sail in the direction of the

Falklands and if, as it was thought, it was not found to be a military exercise, an Argentine invasion was imminent. He called for the Falkland Islands Defence Force to report to the drill hall in Stanley to be briefed by the small detachment of Royal Marines that were stationed at Moody Brook Barracks on the outskirts of the town. The Royal Marines had been stationed on the islands since 1966 and apart from claiming some very beautiful local ladies to return to the UK with, they would train members of the local Defence Force. In addition they would travel throughout the islands teaching farmers how to shoot and also how to dodge bullets. I can recall when we lived at Douglas Station, wild cats would be trapped and released for target practice in preparation of a training visit. Despite most escaping, I can't imagine such acts of cruelty being tolerated today.

So there on the island on that April day in 1982, around 60 Royal Marines, 11 sailors and a group of volunteers from the Falklands Defence Force were all that stood between our homeland and the invaders. I feared this was a mission that, by any stretch of the imagination, could not end well for the defenders.

As the invasion neared, the local radio presenter continued to update us in real time until that is, he explained, an Argentine soldier was pointing a loaded gun to his head and he felt, under the circumstances, he should obey his commands.

The British Marines and the local Defence Force did their best to delay the inevitable, but it was only a matter of time. Despite experiencing more casualties than they will ever admit, Argentine amphibious forces overcame the small garrison of defenders and headed in to Stanley.

As often happens when you're on the losing side, albeit temporarily, I feel very little recognition has ever been given to those brave men who gave their very best to protect the Falklands, knowing the odds were stacked against them.

The next day my mate and I decided to travel 61 miles from Goose Green to Stanley by motorbike to collect our girlfriends and bring them out of the town that now had Argentine occupancy. On the way there we had to cross a fast running river that swells when it rains. On the return trip we had to wade through the water that was now just below the bonnet of a land rover that was making the crossing. At this point we came across my grandfather and several others who explained children were being evacuated from Stanley and they were making the journey to collect them and bring them out to the farms.

As we arrived back at Goose Green we were horrified to see the Argentines were now occupying the farm we had left just hours before. Helicopters were whirring above our heads, landing and spewing out soldiers to take up positions in and around the farm. We stopped at the farm perimeter and discussed whether or not to go into hiding at an empty shepherd's house about 12 miles away. We had no weapons and no military experience. There would also be little food and essential supplies and so the girls voiced their opinions that going in to hiding was not likely to be a good solution. We agreed we should head in to the farm, it's where the masses were and it made sense to join the crowd, after all, despite the Argentine military presence, the farm workers appeared to be continuing to go about their business.

And that's how it was. For a few weeks we were told to carry on 'as normal' under the watchful eyes of the soldiers, but life was far from normal. Each morning they would hold a parade and raise the Argentine flag whilst playing their national anthem loudly. We were placed under curfew and told if anyone was seen out after dark they would be shot. The Argentine soldiers frequently asked for our farm vehicles, but the farm manager and farm hands managed to resist by making excuses and immobilising many of the vehicles. The occupying troops soon started stealing food from the gardens - eggs, chickens and meat from the special store each house had built next to the property. We had no fridges at that time, so meat was hung in fly-proof sheds to prevent the flies getting to it.

The situation continued to worsen. A grass airfield, just outside the farm, was used by the Islander aircraft several times a week to deliver mail, a doctor or someone visiting or leaving the islands. The Argentines were now occupying this area and had around 10 Skyhawks and a Pucara based there to allow them to put good air defence protection in place. One morning they blew up a small tussock, a small island of grass in the bay; the reason is still a mystery unless it was to test the napalm that they were later to attempt to use on the advancing British Paratroopers.

By now, British Prime Minister Margaret Thatcher had authorised a military operation to retake the islands and we understood a British task force comprising warships, submarines and merchant ships, was on its way.

CHAPTER 5

Captivity

Just before 8am on 1st May I stood looking out of a kitchen window as the first two British fighter planes flew in, skimming the water before rising above my former boarding school and then striking the airfield below them, destroying all of the Argentine planes. That move changed things dramatically for us. Within 30 minutes of that raid and well before the smoke had settled, we were all rousted from our houses at gunpoint and herded into the community hall in the middle of the farm. Argentine soldiers were posted around the hall and if anyone dared to look out of a window the soldiers would menacingly point their weapons directly at them, gesturing to them to move away. There were 115 of us: men, women and children. As the day went on it became obvious we wouldn't be going home for dinner. Little did we know then, that some of us would remain in that hall for 29 nights. We were civilian prisoners of war held against our will by the invading Argentine forces, who broke every rule under the Geneva Convention in doing so. The Argentines guessed we would have a means of communication somewhere and suspected at least one of us had managed to make contact with the outside world, perhaps even with the British Armed Forces and they were in no way going to allow that. It would quite likely have been curtains for anyone found to be in possession of a VHF transmitter. Our houses were searched but no transmitters were found. Luckily those owning one had thought ahead and had the ingenuity to hide it outside the house in case exactly this situation arose. With us now locked away, the soldiers then started moving in to our homes.

Holed up in the community hall, someone managed to find an old radio in the back of a cupboard and after some repair work we were able to secretly listen to the BBC World Service. A couple of men would listen to it very quietly, so as not to alert the guards and would then relay the news to everyone else. Unfortunately, we learned one of the two British Harriers we had witnessed attack the airfield had been shot down and the pilot had not survived. This for me and I guess many others, was a very sad moment as the realisation hit that some of our liberators were going to be maimed or die to save our lives and return our freedom.

"We are all in this together and we are all equal" had been the opening words of the general manager when we first found ourselves holed up together in the community hall under the watchful eyes of our captors. We were later to discover some were more equal than others, but in general, taking into consideration not everyone necessarily liked each other prior to captivity, while we were locked up together we all managed to get on relatively well.

From the outset we received very little food and what we had was rationed. I can recall feeling the pain of hunger and hearing many of the children crying because they were so hungry. Being confined was also causing much distress to the majority of the people but especially the children. We had no medical supplies. There were only two toilets for us to use and with so much continual use they would often get blocked, quite unpleasant for all concerned, but eventually one chap was permitted to go outside to unblock us. Being locked up with so many people in a confined space is not easy at any time, but the added uncertainty of what the future held for us made it even more daunting. One morning we were told that all children under the age of 15 would be moved out and taken to Argentina. The parents were horrified; they would lay their lives down for their children. The parents told our captors in no uncertain terms they would have to shoot them first before any child was taken anywhere. The plan was put on hold but the threat remained and had to be lived with.

Luckily enough, one of the men among us could converse in Spanish and he was able to strike up conversations with the Argentine soldiers guarding us. He managed to negotiate the supply of more food and basic bedding to help our miserable existence. He also played an important role later in the surrender negotiations, but was never officially recognised for this. This same gentleman went on to negotiate permission for a couple of the ladies to cook food under guard in the cookhouse, the place where my mother had worked in peace time.

We found a film projector in the hall, it was the projector used to show films on Wednesday and Sunday nights at various locations on the island before the invasion. The films would be circulated around the farms by the Islander plane or overland by Land Rover. With little else to do I volunteered to get it going and used it to show the three films we found in the hall. It was an opportunity for me to get some time alone in the dark for an hour or so and after a couple of weeks I used this time to change my girlfriend. Given our circumstances it was an appalling thing to do. I am to this day lucky to have survived that one and I am truly sorry.

After two weeks as prisoners of war we were allowed outside the front of the hall for a short time to stretch our legs. This was done under heavy guard and came to an abrupt end as soon as the Argentines heard the British had landed on the island. Still secretly listening to the BBC World Service we learned of the successful raid on Pebble Island by the SAS (Special Air Services) and SBS (Special Boat Service) and then of the British landing at San Carlos, Port San Carlos - Blue Beach and Green Beach. Ironically enough it was the Parachute Regiment that made the first beach landings in the Falklands, something Royal Marines normally practice at. Blue Beach was named after 2nd Battalion, Parachute Regiment (2 Para) colours and Green Beach after 3rd Battalion, Parachute Regiment (3 Para), I rather like this. We heard on the BBC World News that 2 Para had advanced towards Goose Green and they were at a house called Camilla Creek, about five miles from Goose Green, preparing to retake the farm.

Unfortunately the Argentines also listened to the BBC World Service and now alerted to the situation, prepared themselves for the imminent attack by British forces. We had been kept awake by gunfire on many occasions during our captivity but on this one night it reached a completely different level. The noise was indescribable and thousands of tracer rounds could be seen. As it continued, I wondered if anyone involved in the battle could possibly survive the night. Because the Argentines had failed to comply with the Geneva Convention in protecting us and indentifying, for outsiders to see, there were civilian prisoners in the hall, we feared for our safety. We had no idea if our liberators knew we were locked in the hall and we knew that one shell or machine gun fire though the walls could wipe us out. With that in mind many of the prisoners crawled under the floorboards of the tin and timber hall in an attempt to feel a little safer.

The Argentines had placed their artillery amongst the farm buildings including the houses, making it more or less impossible for the Brits to strike without destroying half the farm.

As daylight came, we were relieved we remained intact. I climbed up into the steeple to get a better view, only to see the top of the hall strafed with gunfire and an Argentine soldier lying shot and wounded, this led to my very immediate rapid descent. Looking out of the window I could see Darwin Boarding School, previously evacuated, clouded in smoke, flames leaping high from all angles. My heart jumped for joy, I was absolutely delighted... the times I'd dreamt of burning down that school which held so many bad memories and now it was glowing. I found out later the Argentines had snipers within the school, probably lying at window height on a bed in the dorms and the Paras were taking casualties. As a result, the Paras mortared it until it fell silent.

CHAPTER 6

Horrors of war

The farm was liberated on 28th May, by which time some of the farm management and their friends had negotiated their way out of captivity and were already back in their houses. The speech delivered to us by the general manager 28 days earlier about all being equal and in this together ran through my head, so much for that! A huge relief flooded over us all, after 28 days as prisoners of war we were about to be freed. The battle wasn't without its casualties though. Among them was Lieutenant Colonel H Jones, Commanding Officer (CO) of 2 Para, who was severely wounded and subsequently died of his injuries, before he could be evacuated. I believe he remains buried in San Carlos Cemetery. Lt Richard Nunn, the helicopter pilot who was tasked with evacuating the CO was also killed and his co-pilot severely injured when his Scout helicopter was attacked by an Argentine Pucara aircraft as they took off from Camilla Creek House. We later discovered around 17 Paras were also killed, with many more wounded in this battle. Each and every one of us from the Falklands remains deeply indebted for the sacrifices made by the military personnel in liberating us.

We learned Major Chris Keeble had now assumed command of 2 Para and had given the Argentine soldiers the clear message they were overrun, surrounded by British troops and should surrender if they were to avoid huge losses. The reality however was the opposite. 2 Para had in fact taken on an enemy force that had been preparing its defences on high ground for six weeks with three times the numbers of soldiers than the British had. The British soldiers had just tabbed (tactical advance to battle – speed marching with full kit) 20 miles over Sussex Mountain just to get there with no air support or missiles, not forgetting the BBC eliminating any chance of surprise by announcing their exact position to the whole bloody world. The huge bluff was probably their only chance of success and it worked. The Argentine troops surrendered.

They asked for and were given time to collect their belongings before mustering to hand over their weapons.

Back at the hall, I noticed we no longer had guards outside. Looking over my shoulder as I went, I tentatively headed outside to check on my motorbike having last seen it going into a garage opposite the hall. I checked the garage out, there was no-one in there so I entered. I could see from the belongings scattered around, the Argentines had obviously been using the outbuilding. I picked up a discarded 9mm pistol and a big fleece lined Argentine military coat, which I was just about to try on for size, when the door opened and an Argentine soldier burst in. I could tell by the look on his face and the way he pointed his pistol at me, the coat was his. I gripped my pistol hard, ready to take my chances if I had to, but neither of us pulled the trigger. He took the coat and exited. I left carrying a British flying suit which it turned out belonged to the pilot who was shot down on that 1st May raid. It felt disrespectful to just leave it discarded in the garage.

Returning to the hall, the Paras and a small band of Royal Marines were getting hugs from the Kelpers and passing around what little alcohol we had to give, when a helicopter landed. A reporter jumped out, all clean and shiny and approached a British officer, saying: "This is great, were shall we start then?" The reporter soon found himself pinned by the throat to the side of the hall while it was explained to him in no uncertain terms how he and reporters like him, had been responsible for the loss of many soldiers' lives, referring to the BBC broadcast the previous evening disclosing the advance. The reporter was sent on his way with his tail between his legs.

Over the past 28 days the Argentine soldiers, after locking us up, had moved into our houses with no regard or respect for us or our properties or our possessions. They had stolen anything of value and destroyed personal effects and furniture.

After their surrender they had been allowed back into the houses to collect their belongings, something that was hugely disrespected by them. Before collecting their personal items they defecated in the bath and urinated on our beds, they cut up our clothes and to finish up they booby trapped children's toys and left cups on sinks and tables placed upside down with hand grenades inside and the pin out.

I made my way to the house I'd lived in. On entering my own room, I was about to pull the urine soaked mattress from my bed when an accompanying Para noticed a grenade hanging from the springs below. Had he not acted so quickly, we would have both been killed for sure.

My house was used as the first head quarters for 2 Para with the CO taking his first bath since landing at Blue Beach in there. Despite having been locked in the hall for 28 nights, some of us gave up our much longed-for home comforts that evening and stayed one more night in the hall for our liberators, allowing them to use our homes for whatever they needed.

55

The galley of the house had three large coal fires and the army cooks soon took advantage of them. In no time they were churning out hot food for all, including the civilians. My mother got stuck in and helped and even directed the procedures at times, rank was off no consequence to her!

The farm management wasted no time in ordering the farm workers back to work, leaving the women to manage the children and homes, salvaging what they could and making the best of the carnage left in and around the houses by the Argentine soldiers.

The Argentines, now prisoners themselves, were placed into the sheep shearing shed at the edge of the Goose Green farm. Despite the fact when we were locked in the hall the Argentines did not adhere to the rules of the treatment of prisoners, as set out in the Geneva Convention, the British, quite rightly so, played by the rules. The Geneva Convention states that all prisoners of war must be protected and so PoW was painted across the roof of the shearing shed, to warn any Argentine attackers their own people were inside. Something we did not have the luxury of when we were holed up in the hall. The Argentine soldiers failed to indicate the hall contained prisoners of war, which meant we could quite easily have been bombed by our own troops who would not have any idea we were in there.

The Argentine prisoners would be taken from the shed each day to form working parties to clean up around the farm. Some were even made to clean up some of the mess they had left behind.

I was tasked with driving the tractor and trailer used to collect dead Argentine soldiers from the battlefield. In one week we collected 39 bodies which were to be placed in a temporary grave in Darwin horse paddock. At 17-years-old I was driving this tractor around with my 9mm pistol on my hip, alongside a Para sergeant. We would collect a working party of prisoners in the morning and drive around picking up the dead bodies. After collecting the first four I reversed up to the grave and started to tip the trailer when the padre and others screamed at me to stop. It was deemed a callous cold act and I was told the bodies would be taken by the prisoners and lowered in to the grave, giving the procedure some dignity at least; they were certainly "not to be tipped". After all we had been through and me still being in my youth, I had not considered the dead men any different to dead sheep. It's ironic that we had been instructed to treat the bodies with this respect as we then watched with our own eyes as the prisoners lowering their dead into the grave, stole wallets, watches, and wedding rings from the corpses. As the days went on it became difficult to identify the bodies. We found that many of the dead didn't have identity tags and when none were present we needed to rely on driving licenses or the contents of wallets, but as their own brothers had robbed them of such items it was near impossible to indentify some of the bodies.

The prisoners were also used to move the ammunition they had left behind to safer locations. They had left a stack next to the shearing shed where they were now held and again, taking the responsibility of adhering to the rules of the Geneva Convention to protect prisoners very seriously, it was deemed wise to move the ammo in case, during one of the many Argentine air raid attacks on areas of the Falklands not yet liberated, they decided to have a pop at Goose Green.

During one of those many air raids, one evening I placed myself at the corner of our house with an Argentine Belgium FN rifle in my hands and watched an enemy plane zip overhead as it returned to Argentina after its attack on another part of the island. I knew it was not my place to fire in anger at the plane overhead but it felt good, knowing that I could if the need were to arise. The possibility of being actively involved in the fighting, in the defending of my home and people, somehow made me feel better.

The next morning as I approached the tractor to start work, a nearby prisoner, tasked with helping to move the ammo the Argentine soldiers had strategically placed around the farm to safer sites, picked up a shell from the pile to expose and disturb a device that immediately exploded. The soldier was on fire from head to toe, his insides exposed. A leg flew through the air and landed with a thud next to me. I felt the thud but didn't hear it, such was the noise of the explosion; the blast rang in my ears for days. Five died. I felt numb. I struggled to understand how whoever booby trapped that stack of ammunition could stand by and watch his own brothers get blown up. Then again, I couldn't understand why they would want to blow children apart by booby trapping their toys, but that's what they had attempted to do and the only reason they didn't succeed was down to the skills and professionalism of the British forces on the ground at Goose Green.

I later collected the five dead and drove them to join the others in the temporary mass grave.

While we continued clearing up at Goose Green the war raged on. 3 Para had left Green Beach and tabbed sixty miles across the North of East Falklands to Estancia in preparation of mounting an infantry attack to retake Mount Longdon, which would go

onto become one of the bloodiest battles
of the war.

More loss of British life came with the
attack on Royal Fleet Artillery (RFA)
support ships Sir Galahad and Sir Tristram,
bombed by Argentine jets on 8th June. To
support an assault on Stanley, the two
RFAs were due to deliver troops to nearby
Bluff Cove but they anchored off Fitzroy,
five miles short of their original
destination. The Welsh Guards were
waiting to move on to their original
destination and so didn't disembark at
Fitzroy, which is where the Argentines
spotted them and launched an air strike
with devastating consequences.

There were many civilians who assisted in
our liberation during the war, from
transporting ammunition to retrieving the
wounded from the front line during battle;
others risked their lives by sabotaging the
enemy - cutting communication cables,
taking photos and disabling vehicles, while
others buried the dead. Not all were, or
have ever been, recognised for their
bravery when others who contributed far
less have been hailed heroes, but that is

the way of the world I guess, in every catastrophe there is opportunity.

I have no doubt that had the United Kingdom not decided to retake the Falkland Islands in 1982, the approximate 2000 inhabitants would have joined the many thousands of people already missing in Argentina and the world would have soon forgotten us, the Kelpers.

CHAPTER 7

Bound for UK

Looking back on my life I probably had all the makings of becoming a complete psychopath, but thankfully I didn't. I was, however, very angry as a young man. I had learned to use my fists at a very young age, mostly to protect my mother from my stepfather when he so often arrived home drunk. I was angry I had to do this.

However I was also angry I was sent away from my family; I was angry that I was so often left at school while my brother went home for the weekend; I was angry I was abused; I was angry I'd been humiliated; I was angry because the Argentines tried to take my homeland and that's just touching the surface! Did I have post-traumatic stress disorder (PTSD)? If I didn't, I reckon I should have.

I have been blessed with five wonderful children in this life and I always say to them, bad thoughts are an animalistic instinct; only acting upon them causes the grief. Always walk away when you can, but if you really can't, then fight to win.

The British continued to battle Argentine troops, intent on retaking Port Stanley and at 21:00 hours on 14th June 1982 Argentine commander General Mario Menéndez, his troops surrounded and cut off by the British forces, surrendered to Royal Marines commander Major General Jeremy Moore.

Following the surrender helicopters travelled freely to and from Goose Green. I had a yearning to travel to, what we called home, the United Kingdom, and join the British Army. As if at the tender age of 17-years-old I hadn't already seen enough horror and sorrow.

I made my intentions clear and before long I was jumping in to the seat of a forces' helicopter at Stanley to meet a British Military Captain whose job, I guess, was to see if I would even make the first parade. I am not sure what the officer reported back after my interview but it wasn't long before I was on my way to the UK.

I said goodbye to my mother and girlfriend in a field next to the Governor's house in Stanley, climbed aboard a Wessex helicopter and disappeared into the low lying fog. We landed on the deck of the Norland, which was anchored offshore. The Norland was a P & O car ferry that had been requisitioned as a troops and supplies ship and was then used to repatriate the defeated Argentine soldiers. I had to pay for my own passage to the UK of £248, which the Falkland Islands Government has never reimbursed me for and frankly why would they want to? I was given a cabin, as I was one of only a few who had paid for the privilege, and it felt rather posh. I had always suffered with sea sickness and any thoughts I may have had about being alright on a big ship soon diminished. The Norland rolled like a pig and I'm sure I nearly died. I was so sick for the whole three days we were sailing. I thought about the Norland taking the Argentine prisoners back home and couldn't help hoping they had felt as sick as I did. We eventually arrived at Ascension Island and not a moment too soon as far as I was concerned. Thankfully the onward travel to the UK would now be by aeroplane.

The wait on Ascension Island before the next part of our journey was filled with catching fish through the portholes and generally talking war. The captain would make announcements over the intercom from time to time, issuing instructions and one time announcing the Royal Military Police would be coming onboard to search for contraband. For a good hour there was scurrying about the ship with continual splashes on both sides, as those on board discarded any belongings they should not have had on them. Then after all that, the police didn't even show up! I had few possessions personally: a pair of Argentine military boots on my feet, two pairs of jeans, two shirts, a woolly jumper and a fake leather biker jacket with black tassels hanging down each arm, which I thought was really cool.

My turn to climb onboard the RAF DC10 came - it was time to head onwards to the UK. I had flown before on a float plane, but this was no float plane! Everyone sat facing backwards. Apparently if you fall out of the sky facing the rear of a plane from 30,000ft you have a better chance of survival – that's what they told me anyway and that was good enough for me - no more questions! We landed in Senegal to refuel and were asked to disembark onto the runway. We were moved a short distance away from the plane just in case it blew up. The Senegal sun was scorching, I had never experienced heat like it in my life, I thought I would melt. It was made worse by the fact I was wearing my cool looking coat with the tassels - I was convinced it would be stolen if I took it off, everyone seemed to be eyeing it up.

We landed at RAF Brize Norton where it had been arranged for me to be greeted by my aunt and uncle, who I hadn't seen since I was 11. My aunt was one of the pretty local girls who had married a Royal Marine, stationed at Moody Brook Barracks in the Falklands and brought back to the UK. On exiting the plane door we were faced with hundreds of people waiting to greet us. I waved and smiled at them all, shaking hands with them as I waded through all these unbelievably welcoming, friendly people, until my aunt recognised me and reined me in. My aunt and uncle had a shiny blue Ford Escort and we were soon driving smoothly away from RAF Brize Norton towards their home in Street, Somerset. En route they explained to me that the British public are not usually so demonstrative or so overwhelmingly friendly towards strangers but they had all been there to meet their own loved ones – hence the jubilant mood. I wasn't convinced; they seemed pretty pleased to welcome us all, including me.

I very soon discovered, once in the UK, that I was as green as grass - the Falkland Islands' equivalent to Crocodile Dundee. I had been catapulted in to a world that was alien to me. When I first saw the A Team on TV (remember we hadn't had such modern luxuries as TVs), I asked why they hadn't sent these guys to the Falklands to help with the war!

I would walk to the corner shop from my aunt and uncle's house saying "good morning" to everyone I saw. That's what we did back home, greet everyone we came in to contact with, they were after all our neighbours. Within a few weeks I had got to know half the town of Street, while the other half thought I was some kind of head case and avoided me at every opportunity.

My uncle took me to Marks and Spencer to upgrade my very limited wardrobe and soon after, my coat with the tassels went missing; he obviously didn't get my attachment to it. Strangely I was now getting about looking rather like my uncle, who worked in the office at the Clarks shoe factory. With few friends or associates of my own age, my uncle organised for a mate's son to take me to a nightclub in Shepton Mallet. I went along dressed like I had just left the office. My new mates and I stood at the bar, while girls danced around their handbags on the dance floor. I was more than a bit puzzled, girls didn't need to dance around handbags were I came from. Growing up we kids were taught dances like the foxtrot and waltz by our elders but we learned the twist too. I was partial to a bit of dancing and so decided to join the handbags. I cleared the floor and strangely I was never asked out with those guys again.

It was hard to make friends. I had nothing in common with kids of my own age and wasn't able to talk about the things they did, having been brought up in a very different world to the one in which they had been raised.

I had passed my motorbike driving test at the age of 17 in Port Stanley by driving around town in front of a police vehicle, not having to worry about traffic lights or roundabouts as there were none. The licence came in the form of a small book and a policeman ticked the type of licence you has passed a test for. Everyone knew you and knew which test you had taken so you couldn't pull a fast one out there. In the UK however, it was a completely different kettle of fish. I pulled out my licence book and ticked the rest of the boxes, giving myself an instant full car driving licence. I bought myself a mini with the money I had by now received from a war claim for my motorbike, which hadn't been seen since that day I'd checked on it straight after the liberation of the farm at Goose Green. Out on the road my driving skills left a lot to be desired, a little erratic would be an understatement. I stopped to offer anyone who was going in my direction a lift, I often got lost and I was tooted and shouted at a lot, but I soon got the hang of things.

By the way, just for the record, the army later made sure I took and passed a regular British driving test before they let me loose in any of their vehicles!

I was acutely aware of the sacrifices that had been made to save me and my fellow Kelpers during the Falklands War and I had nothing else to offer in exchange apart from myself. Joining the British Forces was my way of giving something back and so I headed to the Army Careers office to set in stone the promise I had made to myself and my reason for coming to the UK.

I had already accepted my limited level of education (remember I was supposed to spend my life farming on the island) wouldn't get me to Sandhurst, but hoped I could at least make the first parade somewhere. On taking the entrance exam my options were limited but I aimed high and signed up to join the Parachute Regiment. Next was the physical and after the short test I was left in no doubt I needed to get in better shape. Meanwhile I took some short term work on a dairy farm in Somerset, driving tractors and milking cows, something I could do standing on my head and it gave me a few pounds for petrol.

I didn't drink much alcohol; a couple of 'Toby tops' was my limit. I remember the first time I ordered one, the barmaid wasn't sure what I meant by a "point of Toby" but quickly worked out that I was trying to say pint. The accent of the Falklands is quite similar to that of New Zealand, we tend to pronounce the H as in Notting Ham, Birming Ham. In the Falklands we only had tins of beer, nothing on draught and so I'd never had to order a pint of anything, this was one of many new experiences for me.

CHAPTER 8

Giving back

The eventual success of the Falklands War and all the media coverage that accompanied it had resulted in a surge of applications from young men and women to join the British forces. Good on them wanting to fight for their country, but I did wonder if that many of them really knew what they might be letting themselves in for. I had experienced firsthand the violence of war and the devastation it brought, including brutal attacks on the ground with hand to hand fighting, as well as missile strikes, air raids and more.
As a result of the increased interest the Paras now had an 18-month waiting list, however my application was processed and I was fast tracked into training.
The press, by now, had somehow found out I had travelled over from the Falklands to join the British Army and were very

keen to interview me. I had been told in no uncertain terms on signing up, that as a soldier I should not be discussing things with the press and telling my story via the media. The press were very insistent towards me, insisting people have a right to know what it was like and hear about the horrors of living through a war. I remember suggesting people could always join the army if they wanted to know. I am still of that opinion today. As far as front-line fighting goes, military units have enough on their plate in times of war without wet nursing reporters who have no regard for the safety of the troops by giving away their location and putting them in grave danger.

I signed up to the army for six years as I thought at 24 I would still be young enough to do something else if the army wasn't working out. I served in the UK, Falklands, Denmark, Italy, Netherlands, Germany and Canada with the Parachute Regiment and Royal Artillery. I even made Lance Corporal.

During a cadre course one of the soldiers attempted to take his own life, first by drinking Brasso and then slitting his wrists. He didn't succeed. I was given the task of cleaning up the blood as they said: "Browning you've been bloodied so you clean it up." No-one ever asked then or after if I was okay. There was definitely a 'man up and get on with it' attitude, with no time for acknowledging the possibilities of PTSD.

Unfortunately I wasn't to keep my rank of Lance Corporal. I had been agitated by another soldier while serving in Italy and we had come to blows. It resulted in him being taken to hospital and me being taken in to police custody. The Italian police wrote a fourteen page statement in Italian and told me to sign it. I couldn't read Italian and so I refused which resulted in me being badly beaten by the police and thrown in to jail. I retaliated by lashing out, which resulted in them restraining me by sticking a 9mm pistol in my mouth with the hammer back. Once my unit recovered me I was driven directly out of Italy and was demoted as a result of my antics. What I had faced in custody, the horror of the treatment I received was never talked about. Once again I was expected to just get on with things.

Some of the military returning from the Falklands, like many who have experienced war firsthand, suffered terribly, psychologically. A large proportion of them are still coping with it today, while others have taken and are still taking their own lives. The care available for those suffering from PTSD was unfortunately, at that time, non-existent as far as I could see. Wars like the Falklands continue to claim lives, well after the battles have been won.

Despite the odd hiccup I served my six years with pride, still intent on giving back. So deep is my gratitude, in whatever I do to this day, I try to ensure I give something back, whether that is to my country, my community, to charities or to my friends and family.

During leave I had often stayed with my grandfather's brother, my great uncle and his wife in the English county of Berkshire. They were good people. Through them I met the young lady who was to become my first wife. It was all a bit quick but our relationship was like a rollercoaster ride and we just got swept along. Despite nagging doubts this might be lust rather than everlasting love, we married a year before I left the army. We had a terrible start to our marriage; her father died of a heart attack the day after our wedding and we were scheduled to travel straight over to Germany where I was based. She found herself grieving in a different country without family and friends, with me away much of the time. It wasn't easy for her to get over the loss of her father, feeling very much alone in alien surroundings. When it comes to personal loss, I have learned over the years that you don't learn to live with it; you must learn to live without it. There are only two sure things in life, death and taxes and in my opinion they both hurt.

My military career came to a natural end after my six years. I had trained hard for a commando course but I walked away after just two weeks, my heart was simply no longer in it and you need to be 100% committed in this line of duty or you become a danger to yourself and to others. I had lost momentum and motivation and felt my life's journey now needed a change of direction. I left feeling that I had now, at least, given something back.

CHAPTER 9

New beginnings

After leaving the army, because of my military background, my wife and I were given a council flat in Buckinghamshire, her home county. I got work in the building trade and life went on. Before long our first child, Shane, came in to the world. I cut the umbilical cord, as I did for all five of my children. It was an amazing feeling. It was a very proud moment, one of the very special moments a father shares with the mother of his child. I had never experienced feelings like the ones I experienced each time one of my children was born. The birth of my first child definitely stirred emotions in me that had been buried very deep, if they had ever previously existed at all. I'm pretty sure this was the first time I really felt love. The love I had for that tiny baby is indescribable, along with the feeling of this huge responsibility for something so precious. It's how I felt after the birth of each and every one of my children.

When an aunt decided she wanted to move from her council house we were lucky enough to do an exchange with her. We moved in to a three bedroom house, still in Buckinghamshire, with me working as a ground worker picking up contracts wherever I could. By working hard, I managed to save a deposit and secure a mortgage to buy our home from the council. Life wasn't easy, I was working much of the time, and the relationship between me and my wife wasn't great. She felt a second child might bring us closer together and before long it was confirmed our second child was on the way.

Life should have been sweet, but it wasn't. I continued to struggle with emotions of any kind and many of them were replaced with anger. I still had a lot of anger buried deep inside me which would often surface more easily than it should. Once again however, I felt this deep love, when our daughter, my only daughter, Stacie was born. Here was another beautiful human being who my wife and I had created, but despite this I didn't feel settled. The longer the marriage continued, the more obvious it became that my wife and I had little in common; there was no chemistry, no connection and very little deep and meaningful conversation, but without doubt there were two lovely children. As I fought to keep my frustrations at bay, I thought back to my terrible upbringing and knew I wanted better for my children. I didn't want my frustrations and anger issues to affect my children and I certainly didn't want them growing up in an unhappy home, so I did something I am not proud of... I walked out on my wife and two kids, with nothing but a black bag with a few clothes in and my Nissan pick-up that was two months behind on the hire purchase (HP) repayments. Stacie was only a few months old, Shane just three. My wife soon found a new partner. I was pleased for her and hoped she would be happy. I still wanted to be a part of my children's lives but that proved more difficult than it should have been. I offered money but she just wanted the house. No problem, I signed the house over to my wife and her new partner, I took nothing from it. Seeing the children was sporadic and at one time I had to get the courts involved to ensure visits were maintained, however I had to understand they had their own lives now and seeing my children became more and more infrequent. Moving forward I paid money when they needed it but I missed out on building any kind of relationship with my children.

It was now time to look to the future. I needed to find me and then make sure I was the best version of me that I could be. I needed to do it for myself and I needed to make sure I could be there for my children, Shane and Stacie, in the future if and when they wanted me.

I continued to work in the building trade and it was while I was working on a job in Buckinghamshire, for a lady called Debbie, that I met the first real love of my life, the mother of my next three children, carer of 12 horses, two donkeys, a few chickens and a dog called Barney; they all came later.

Debbie supplied horses and period carriages to the film industry and Claire, who adores horses, had been working for her as a film stand in on horseback. She'd doubled for actresses like Sharon Stone and had ridden horses and worked as a horse handler in films like Robin Hood Prince of Thieves and Sense and Sensibility among others. We got talking about her love of horses. Luckily I knew a fair bit about horses myself, having been riding in the Falklands since I could walk. I loved Claire from the minute I first saw her, we got on so well, we even talked about running away to Canada and working with horses together. We both fell, hook line and sinker and I can't remember ever being happier than the day she agreed to be my wife.

I had by now moved in to a shared house and continued working hard to support myself and my estranged family. I still hadn't managed to keep the payments up-to-date on the pick-up and one night, in fact the night before I was moving away, when I returned to the house after work I clocked two 'suits' sitting on the drive. As I got out of the van they approached me: "Mr Browning?" "No" I said, "I just work for him." They continued: "Well we have a repossession order for the pick-up." I kept up the pretence and said I couldn't hand over the keys until Mr Browning got home. Inside the house I asked my housemate to jump in her car and follow me down the drive and around the block, so that when we got back to the house she could drive in behind be. That way, with her parked behind me and a big old tree blocking the other side of my truck, they wouldn't be able to remove the vehicle. The 'suits' sat outside for hours. I even took them a cup of tea and told them Mr Browning was going to be very late. Eventually they turned in, but I knew they'd be back at first light. In the depths of the night I asked my housemate to follow me out of the drive again. I hid the van away from the house and got a lift home with her. When the 'suits' turned up very early, of course the van had gone.

Claire and I had already agreed we would move to her home town of Portishead in North Somerset and stay with her parents Tess and Hopper for a while. I picked up the hidden Nissan later in the day, collected Claire and we drove out of town. I was completely penniless but had the love of my life with me and was sure there would be good times ahead.

Moving to Portishead was supposed to be a temporary measure, until we were ready to follow our Canadian dream but that was not to be. Life took us down a very different path, albeit a pretty good one. Claire now owns and runs a wellbeing centre offering equine facilitated learning for children and young people who need an extra little help with life and she is exceptionally good at it.

Did I have PTSD? Maybe. I was having bad dreams, but I'd always had bad dreams, in fact I still do. I have never been diagnosed with PTSD and I reckon I could convince an assessor either way, but I have learned to control my anger these days. I take time out and write down how I feel or what I want to say and then look for my response as though I was talking to someone else. It's my way of dealing with things and it works for me. I think more people should try it.

I have also learned to deal with horror and stress by treating each trauma as a book. If it falls in front of me from time to time I will read a few pages but then I always try to place that book back firmly on its shelf and move on, only taking it down to read at my convenience if the need arises.

As far as I'm concerned, you either live with the cards you have been dealt or you change them for new ones. I was all for changing them for new ones and I hoped Claire would be with me all the way and was ready for the ride!

CHAPTER 10

The world of tunnelling

We moved in with Claire's parents while we got settled. I looked for work, willing to take anything to get us on our feet and was offered a job as a labourer in the yard of a tunnelling project next to the Avonmouth Bridge, just one junction down the motorway from Portishead. The Irish tunnel foreman, Tommy Gallagher Snr, gave me the start. I'd been working hard there for about six months when Tommy Snr, told me their next job was going to be in London and asked if I would be interested in travelling. I informed him I was from the Falkland Islands. He didn't get that, but I did go to London. I had picked up quite a bit of understanding about the tunnelling industry when working in the yard in Avonmouth and I now moved from yard labourer to miner. I ask a lot of questions, always have. I made my way to the tunnel face by working hard and learning fast, the Irish took no prisoners and carried no passengers when it came to work. I learned the trade from the very best of them and I am very grateful to those men.

Tunnelling operatives build the underground tunnels needed for services such as rail lines, water works and power stations. They assist with the excavation, support and forming of tunnels and shafts. This involves working in the cramped conditions of a tunnel boring machine (TBM) not unlike that of a submarine (although there's no room for passengers), operating the machinery associated with the boring and construction process.

I started work on a power station tunnel that would run under the Thames. Meanwhile Claire had picked up several contracts back on film sets with the horses. It wasn't permanent work, just ad hoc, but it worked for us. She was based back in Buckinghamshire when the contracts came along, so once I'd finished work for the week in London I'd pick her up and we'd return home to Portishead for the weekend, back with Tess and Hopper. Eventually we managed to find someone who had a house to let in Portishead and luckily, despite my credit rating being as low as it possibly could go, the owner trusted me to pay the rent.

The tunnelling contracts came and went, it wasn't consistent work and there were often periods between jobs where there was no work and I had to scrabble around taking labouring work to pay the bills and make ends meet. Life again, was not always easy and London can be a very lonely place when you have little money. When the money wasn't coming in it was tough but I didn't want to worry Claire about it. I'd make sure the bills were paid, even if it meant going without myself. Working in London I'd always say I was staying in digs but occasionally it would be the car. One Sunday night as I said goodbye to Claire and headed back to London she'd packed me a big dish of stew to eat in my accommodation over the next couple of days. Little did she know that at the time I was actually sleeping in the car and so made do living on that lovingly prepared stew, stone cold, for days and I'd pawned my necklace to pay for the petrol to get to back to London and home again the following weekend.

After working on the Barking Reach Power tunnel project we moved on to the Jubilee underground line extension project. I found digs above a bar behind Waterloo Station and shared a room with a guy called John, who was also from Portishead. The room was freezing cold with no heating and we could hear the station's loudspeaker system announcing every train's arrival and departure, day and night. One morning, returning home after night shift, when we got to the side door of the bar I remember seeing one of the big round bins, used for empty beer bottles and cans, was lying on its side. I told John we should stand it up for the landlady. We did so and got a bit more than we bargained for, with loud angry shouts coming from within. It just so happened a tramp had been sleeping in the bin and was enraged that we should be messing with his temporary abode. John said we should get him out, but I persuaded him it would be better to leave him inside to cool down and then get him out later.

When we got into our accommodation we discovered the other workers living in the place had done a runner. Their room had been the only one in the digs that had a heater, so with them now gone John ran in to their room, picked up the heater and jubilant we were going to have some heat, started back to our room with it tucked under his arm. I noticed the lead had gone under the door as he sprinted towards me, I yelled at him to stop but it was too late, the plug caught on the door and the cable pulled out of the heater rendering it useless. Our one chance of getting warm that night was scuppered.

We'd often have a bit of fun among the workforce on that Jubilee Line. One of the lads working on the opposite shift, PJ, would always place the exact change he needed for the Dartford Tunnel toll in his jeans pocket. I saw an opportunity to have a bit of fun one night as we turned up to begin work and he was in the communal showers having just finished his shift. I tie wrapped his coins tight in the bottom of his jeans pocket. When he arrived at the toll he apparently caused quite a queue of cars to build up behind him as he struggled in vain to retrieve the coins from the depths of his pocket. I was amused to discover the next day, that in the end he'd jumped out of his vehicle and dropped his jeans to rub the pocket on the road surface in order to tear the material to get the coins out. This was made even funnier because he'd often go commando and had done so on this occasion which resulted in him baring his butt to the world, or at least the queue of cars behind him.

On another occasion a young engineer had one of the first mobile phones. He was busy showing it off to anyone who would listen. I told him it was my mother's birthday and asked if I could call her to wish her a happy birthday. He proudly handed me the phone. My mother and I had a great chat which lasted about 20 minutes. When I handed the phone back to him and thanked him he asked me where my mother lived. When I said the Falkland Islands the colour drained from his face and he couldn't get any words to come out of his mouth. As I understand it, that call set him back about £200!

As tunnelling didn't offer me consistent work and there were often periods between jobs where there was nothing going in that line of work, I looked around for labouring jobs back in Portishead to pay the bills and make ends meet. I was lucky, I had made some good connections and local contractors Steve, Chris or one of the other good guys based in and around Portishead would normally manage to find a place for me within their workforce, for which I was always grateful. On one occasion, Dave K offered me some groundwork after I'd met him in the Portishead Workingman's Club. I explained I was waiting on a call for a tunnelling job but he still gave me the start. I started first thing on Monday morning, a very rainy Monday morning at that. 90 minutes in I got the call to drop everything and go tunnelling in London and that's what I did. Dave was a very understanding bloke! Tunnelling contracts continued to come and go and I continued to find myself in poor living conditions in London. The arrangement continued for years, although as the money improved so did my temporary accommodation.

Back home, Claire had given up work and gave birth to our first son Kyle. Working away and only seeing them at weekends wasn't ideal but I was intent on building a good life for us, carving out a future, and that was the price we had to pay. I had now managed to get a mortgage, having borrowed a deposit from my step-brother Kevin and his wife Chantelle. We had set up home in a Victorian semi-detached house in Portishead just a few doors up from Alan and Max, who had become really good friends and close to what is now one of my favourite social meeting places, the Phoenix Bar. It was good to have a place to call home, a proper home and even better to have great friends right on your doorstep (well, more or less). While I was away, I was completely focussed on work; then it was good to get home and catch up with Claire and build a relationship with my son.

In 1998 I got a call from a German engineer, Dietmar, who I'd got to know when we were working on the Jubilee Line project for the London Underground. He was working on a large tunnelling project in Westerschelde, in the south western area of the Netherlands and he asked if I would like to go over to work with him. It would give me more experience and the money wasn't bad so I agreed. I set off for Netherlands in an old Saab and before I'd even reached Dover the exhaust had dropped off. I bodged it at a service station and managed to get on the ferry in one piece, however as the car dropped off the ramp in Calais so did the exhaust.

I made it to the jobsite without being arrested and went to work. As it turned out they needed more experienced labour so I called some of the gang I'd previously worked with and 26 of them decided to take up the opportunity.

We were employed by the large German company Phillip Holzman, which employed 40,000 people around the world. As it was a large reputable company you would think we would be in good hands but that wasn't the case. Firstly at the time we Brits were used to being paid weekly and in Europe they paid monthly, so even though the beer was cheap most of us were on an extremely tight budget to begin with. After a while that four weeks 'til pay day turned to six, which put us all a bit on edge as well as making us strapped for cash. Then came the bad news, it was just a few weeks before Christmas and we were told there would be no pay coming as the company had ceased trading with mounting debts. By then we had formed two strong teams, one of which I was the foreman for. So there we were, I had persuaded 26 men to join me from England and Ireland, it was nearly Christmas, we hadn't been paid for six weeks and it didn't look as though we were going to get paid. As if that wasn't bad enough it looked as though the project would close down, at least for a while. To say I wasn't very popular would be an understatement. We did what British people often do in times of crisis; we went to the bar to discuss our next move. I stood nose to nose with the other tunnel foreman Hugh, as he made it quite clear how everyone held me personally responsible for the predicament we found ourselves in. To be honest he was right. I'd seen the warning signs and had thought it might be coming, but had hoped it wouldn't end like this. At one point our conversation got a bit heated but I took control and explained to Hugh that we had enough on our plate without he and I rolling about on the floor. One thing I was sure of though, if we packed our bags and left now, before being officially dismissed, we would definitely not get any money. I said if he could get the lads back to the UK I would stay behind and do my best to bring the money back. He agreed.

I managed to find a solicitor who was sympathetic to our situation and just happened to have an emphatic dislike of Germans at the time, due to some personal issues he'd experienced. He and I got on well and he agreed to help me, despite the fact I had no money to pay for his services. We arranged a meeting with the project leaders and after some serious negotiating it was agreed they would arrange for a cash payment to cover some of the outstanding wages and I would travel back to the UK with it. We were talking around 80,000 British pounds and I was going to transport it all back to the UK in my suitcase to make sure everyone got paid. Thankfully I had been able to get the exhaust fixed properly on the car, so as long as I wasn't set up to be robbed or pulled over by the police on the way to the ferry, I reckoned I should be okay. During the negotiations with the project leaders we had also agreed that when the project restarted my men could work on it once again.

Back home the look on my bank manager's face was an absolute picture as, three days before Christmas, I entered his office, threw down a big bag filled with £80,000 cash and pressed in to his hand a list of details of 26 different bank accounts, explaining how important it was these men got paid and got paid right now. It was done.

A few months later the project leader called me and said the tunnel had now been taken on by a new company and they were ready for us to go back, however we needed to find a company to work through as they couldn't or wouldn't employ us directly. I contacted Tommy Gallagher Snr, who now had his own company sub-contracting and supplying tunnel personnel and we headed back to Netherlands to negotiate a deal. Unfortunately things didn't work out as planned because the Department of International Trading said Tommy Snr did not have the right licence to work overseas and they couldn't issue one for him within the timeframe required. This was deeply disappointing for me as I held Tommy Snr in very high regard and still do to this today.

Word soon spread within the industry, that I had a team of good men experienced in tunnelling, ready and waiting to take up position on the Dutch project but we needed a contractor to work for who would subcontract us in. I was approached by several different recruitment agencies vying for the contract who were willing to take us on and I realised there was potential to make myself some money here. After all, I had

got the gang together; I'd taken
responsibility for them, especially on
negotiating their money when the project
had shut down before Christmas.

One of the companies that approached me
was the Dutch firm Maritime IPS Powerful
People. They were a big name in supplying
personnel to the maritime industry,
especially dredging, surveying, quality
health and safety and offshore projects.
They had no direct experience of supplying
tunnel workers but seemed to think it
would fit well with their other lines of
contracting. They offered me a better deal
than the other agencies, not necessarily
financially but better terms and
conditions; all the legal stuff was good
with IPS. We did the deal, shook hands and
me and the guys started back on the
project, subcontracted in by IPS.

I discovered immediately that the people
at IPS really were clueless when it came to
tunnelling. They were however very happy
with the margins they were making
financially and approached me to see if I
would help them get more involved in the
tunnelling market. I naively informed

them that apart from a book with the names and numbers of very good tunnelling men, I had very little to offer them. Luckily for me they felt I had sufficient knowledge of the industry to help them out, they needed someone who understood tunnelling and they took a punt on me.

I agreed to go into their office on my free days and take a look at things. In the same breath I also took the opportunity to let them know that I had never used a computer, couldn't spell and swore quite a bit when frustrated. They obviously saw something in me beyond that because those things didn't seem to concern them. My time in their office went well, too well in fact, as I was soon so busy I couldn't get back to the tunnel face.

Through IPS I indentified another tunnelling project in Rotterdam. The Botlekspoor Tunnel was in need of personnel and I secured a dinner meeting with Thomas, the German tunnel manager for the project. He requested we went to a Japanese restaurant, which was promptly organised by one of the IPS secretaries.

Once I'd moved from the Falklands I had learned fast about life outside the islands, however I had yet to experience a Japanese restaurant. I met the tunnelling manager and we proceeded to the restaurant where we were taken to a private room but there were no chairs inside, just a low table and cushions. We had to sit on the cushions on the floor! Quite bizarre I thought. Then came the menu, which seemed even more bizarre to me. I waited to follow my guest, he picked menu A so I chose menu B without having a clue as to what I was about to receive. I'm not a fish lover at the best of times so when a dish of raw fish arrived I decided I wasn't really hungry. Even my guest, who had been the one to choose that we dine in a Japanese restaurant, didn't seem too impressed. We picked our way around eight courses, eating just a little of anything that wasn't still moving and washed it down with beer. At the end we agreed to work together, I with IPS would recruit the tunnelling personal required and subcontract them in. We shook hands and promised any future meetings would

be held in the office and not in a Japanese
restaurant.

CHAPTER 11

Opportunities

Through the Dutch projects in Westerschelde and Rotterdam I was able to demonstrate the ability to supply skilled tunnelling personnel to an international market and made a bit of a name for myself in doing so. This led to me being approached by Herrenknecht AG, a major player in the world of tunnelling. Herrenknecht AG designs and builds tunnel boring machines to facilitate the worldwide infrastructure demand. To offer a full service they required mechanical and electrical specialists and in 1991 they asked if I could provide them with this type of personnel. Of course I could! IPS now offered me a new challenge. They asked me to manage their specially formed tunnelling division; it came with a good salary and profit share and was an opportunity I wasn't going to turn down.

The discussions with Herrenknecht continued and a contract was negotiated and signed between me as head of tunnelling at IPS and Herrenknecht. Getting back home to Claire was less frequent. I went from going home every weekend to getting there about once a month but lucky for me she continued to support me all the way.

My new position with IPS was soon challenged. A company called Gabro had been 'top dogs' in supplying equipment and personnel to the tunnelling industry for more than 10 years and they could see I was now carving out quite a reputation on the personnel side of the things with IPS. Until now, Gabro Tunnelling had been supplying tunnelling personnel to Herrenknecht exclusively. The owners of Gabro invited me to a meeting where they suggested if I wanted a long term career in this industry I really needed to consider joining them. They held their hands up and told me they realised they had taken their eyes off the ball and hadn't seen me coming otherwise they would have stepped in and prevented me from picking up any major contracts. I reported the meeting and its contents to the owners of IPS, who were of course extremely concerned; I think they could see the potential future dividends slipping away. I weighed up my choices: my existing deal with IPS and now a new one on the table with Gabro. I had a major decision to make and not a lot of time to make it in. The conclusion I came to was I needed to see inside the workings of a company that had been so successful in looking after the needs of a field service as big as Herrenknecht. My experience of these companies was at that time limited and expanding that experience had to be a positive move. I informed IPS of my decision and took a plane to Bangkok to meet the owner of Gabro, but not before ensuring the door was still open for me with IPS if the new job didn't work out. We agreed I could return to them having gained additional experience, good or bad, as they knew it would benefit them in one way or another.

The first warning sign for me was on the way back from Bangkok. Gabro had booked me out in business class but the return was cattle class. Back then it wasn't difficult to upgrade with a nice smile and the cost of a crate of Guinness, so I did just that and put it on my expenses tab under taxi and they paid! There was however a principle involved here and I had that clocked.

Looking at the contracting situation I could see huge advantages of the two companies, IPS and Gabro, forming an alliance. I manipulated the cooperation at risk to myself and my position at times. If I overstepped the mark I could have been replaced at any point, should the right person come along. If I'm honest, knowing the bosses of both organisations, I knew the two big companies working together would probably not last, but it was worth a shot. The two companies started working together with me as the glue, but my hunch had been right; the two soon parted company. Gabro operated in a completely different way to IPS and an incident in China had left alarm bells ringing with me and others at IPS. When our alliance dissolved I stayed with IPS while

Herrenknecht withdrew its contract and went on to do a deal with a new Danish agency called Dan Tunnel. As for Gabro, one of the directors decided to return home and retired, while the other went on to work on contracts on the other side of the world before eventually retiring himself.

Dan Tunnel was now breaking into the market supplying mainly Danish skilled tunnel personnel. Something I would have to deal with at a later date. Meanwhile at IPS we had secured a new tunnel project, the Panache Canal, in Netherlands near Nijmegen close to the German border. My challenge was to find 86 people who would work with us on the project. I now needed a right hand to support me in the field and I found Johnny, a Danish chap who I gelled with immediately the minute we met. Johnny went on to be my best man when I married Claire and was my support in the field for 21 years until a car accident forced him to leave the industry. We set about recruiting from the UK and Denmark, advertising in the local papers for people to go underground. I organised open days in both the UK and Denmark and we had 160 people turn up for interviews. We firstly chose the best and then took a gamble on the rest to fill all the vacancies.

While looking for accommodation for the teams we found a hotel in Kleve, just inside the German border, that was in financial trouble. I could see a deal coming that would be mutually beneficial. We offered to take up accommodation in the hotel for all our men on the condition we struck a good price. It was a no brainer for the troubled hotel and so the deal was done.

Having the accommodation set away from the work site would hopefully protect the workers and the company. I didn't want to see British tunnellers drunk in a bar in Nijmegen, although I can't say it never happened. I had previously experienced a situation where Dutch reporters had interviewed a couple of drunk tunnellers working on a German led project in Turnursen, Netherlands. The next day the story and accompanying photo appeared on the front page of the local newspaper, quoting the workers as saying: "Germans are good for nothing but building houses". It didn't go down too well and as a result we had to move on. It reared its head again later and was of great embarrassment to me when the project manager on the Westerschelde job presented it to me just as I was negotiating the money to take back to the UK for the guys. If I could avoid this kind of thing happening again I would.

We rented some vehicles from what we called 'Wreck A Car' rather than 'Rent A Car'. We organised several cars and two buses to transport the teams to and from the hotel and I was a bit taken aback when, within a week, speeding and parking fines started arriving. I gave them to my foreman Johnny telling him to put names to the fines but when they came back the names listed included my name, along with Mickey Mouse and Donald Duck. They thought they were having the last laugh but they obviously didn't know me well. It's not a good idea to underestimate me and I don't take kindly to being taken advantage of. At the end of the project someone asked me what had happened to all those fines and I told him no-one had missed a pound or two taken from their wages every month and the fines had been covered by small deductions from everyone's wages over the past 18 months.

The food in the hotel was another issue and had been from day one. I was confronted about the food by an unhappy employee on one occasion and I said I'd sort it, but apparently he thought I wasn't taking his complaint seriously enough. Next morning I found a pile of excrement placed on a beer mat on the roof of my car. I removed it before driving to the site. I called the young man over and told him we needed to part company after such a childish act. He asked how I'd known it was him, and I said I hadn't been 100% sure, but thanked him for now confirming it. Back at the hotel I wrote a set menu which I knew would be acceptable to the workers and the German chefs followed it to the letter. Thankfully this pacified the workforce.

The project went very well and on the back of it we started a 23-year working relationship with Vinci, a major French company. Next we moved on to Sweden with Vinci and worked on the Hallandsas Railway Tunnel project with them there over a 10-year period.

CHAPTER 12

Onwards and upwards

I secured work with another two tunnel boring machine manufacturers: Robins from America and Canadian company Lovat. I think this is probably what prompted Herrenknecht to get in touch with me once again and I started working with them too, this time supplying personnel world-wide for them.

I had learned a lot from the Dutch, they are masters of trading with a no-nonsense approach and they never seemed to fear making decisions no matter how big, something many other nationalities I have worked with could learn from. On the other hand, I also found the Dutch directors at IPS were capable of robbing me as they failed to pay me the correct amount of profit share we had agreed. I was, however, prepared to turn a blind eye to this for the time being for my own gain, furthering my knowledge and understanding of this new world I was involved in.

IPS began to set up schools to train personnel where there was a skills shortage and I would visit the training places. I once travelled to Indonesia to visit a welding school that IPS had set up. It was about a three hour drive from Jakarta. On the night we arrived at the hotel the bar was full so we went out to a bar in town. On the way back in a taxi we were pulled over by armed police and told to lie face down on the road while they searched the taxi. I thought... here we go again! Whatever they were looking for they didn't find and we were soon on our way back to the hotel.

Herrenknecht had supplied a TBM to the Dublin Port contract in 2001 and we were supplying some of the labour to assemble and install the machine and get the tunnelling project underway. A chap called Pat from Galway, a highly skilled time-served mechanic who wanted to travel the world and reckoned tunnelling might afford him that opportunity, kept calling me asking for a start, even though he hadn't ever worked in tunnelling before. The situation reminded me of Tommy Snr giving me a go all those years ago. After Pat calling me about 100 times I decided, based on his enthusiasm alone, I would give him a go. I contracted him in as a member of the technical team and told him if anyone asked where he had worked previously in tunnelling, to say Germany. The Germans on the site knew full well he had never worked in Germany let alone in a tunnel there, but he proved to be a quick learner and very capable, so they accepted him. Pat is still working for me at GTE and has become one of the most respected senior mechanical superintendents in the tunnelling world.

I did a lot of travelling, with many of my trips providing me with a story or two to tell. One time I drove from Rotterdam to Paris to visit a project we had men working on. After getting lost a few times en route, I found myself stuck in traffic in a tunnel. Suddenly I was shunted from behind. I jumped out of my car and angrily pulled open the door of the car behind me. I was confronted by a little person with an adapted car, smoking a big fat cigar, with a huge grin on his face. He said nothing; nothing at all. He just looked at me, smiled this great big smile and took another tug on his cigar. It seemed surreal, like something out of a hippy movie. I just closed the door, got back in my car and drove on.

Meanwhile Claire was doing a great job raising Kyle who was growing fast. Luckily she had friends and family around her for support. We now had a bit of stability as I had a regular income. I worked hard and then made the most of my time when I got back home.

When I received my first ever profit share from IPS I bought our first piece of land. I think I still had a bit of the farmer in me from my days in the Falklands and buying the land allowed Claire and I to build the dream of keeping horses. Besides, I trust in land and bricks and mortar more than I trust banks and as a result, even to this day, while I am asset rich I am cash poor and probably always will be.

Claire gave birth to our second son Jack in 1999 and then Flynn in 2003. We had discussed our upbringings and how we would parent our own children. Obviously I was determined not to make any of the parental mistakes I had encountered as a child. There is no schooling to become a parent, you learn from your own upbringing and when I say learn, I mean you learn what is good and what is bad from the way you are brought up, from the way you are treated and the way you feel about it. You can take the good and build on it for your own children and as for the bad - you try and make sure they don't go through some of the things you did as a child. I believe the conscience you are born with lets you know when you are being fair and when you're not and when you're being wicked and when you're not. I definitely wanted better for my children. I didn't want them to experience anything like the childhood I'd had, however in my quest to provide for my family and to make them safe and proud, prices have been paid. The song Cat's In The Cradle by Johnny Cash comes to mind. For anyone trying to work out their home life balance, it's well worth checking the song out. Here are the lyrics that stay with me and probably always will:

Cat's In The Cradle

My child arrived just the other day
He came to the world in the usual way
But there were planes to catch, and bills to pay
He learned to walk while I was away
And he was talking 'fore I knew it, and as he grew
He'd say: "I'm gonna be like you, dad
You know I'm gonna be like you."

And the cat's in the cradle and the silver spoon
Little boy blue and the man in the moon
"When you coming home, dad?"
"I don't know when, but we'll get together then
You know we'll have a good time then."

My son turned ten just the other day
He said: "Thanks for the ball, dad, come on let's play
Can you teach me to throw?" I said: "Not today
I got a lot to do." He said: "That's okay"
And he, he walked away, but his smile never dimmed
It said 'I'm gonna be like him, yeah
You know I'm gonna be like him.'

And the cat's in the cradle and the silver spoon
Little boy blue and the man in the moon
"When you coming home, dad?"
"I don't know when
But we'll get together then
You know we'll have a good time then."

Well, he came from college just the other day
So much like a man I just had to say:
"Son, I'm proud of you, can you sit for a while?"
He shook his head, and they said with a smile:
"What I'd really like, dad, is to borrow the car keys
See you later, can I have them please?"

And the cat's in the cradle and the silver spoon
Little boy blue and the man in the moon
"When you coming home, son?" "I don't know
when, but we'll get together then, dad,
You know we'll have a good time then."

I've long since retired, my son's moved away
I called him up just the other day
I said: "I'd like to see you if you don't mind."
He said: "I'd love to, dad, if I can find the time
You see, my new job's a hassle, and the kids have
the flu
But it's sure nice talking to you, dad
It's been sure nice talking to you."
And as I hung up the phone, it occurred to me
He'd grown up just like me, my boy was just like
me.

And the cat's in the cradle and the silver spoon
Little boy blue and the man in the moon
"When you coming home, son?"
"I don't know when but we'll get together then, dad
We're gonna have a good time then.

Songwriters: Harry F. Chapin / Sandy Chapin
Cat's in the Cradle lyrics © Warner Chappell Music, Inc

CHAPTER 13

Moving on

After a four-month tour in the Falklands in 1984 I didn't return to the islands for 19 years. The trip in 2003 wasn't planned, I had memories from the islands that I would rather forget and keep buried away. I returned to attend my grandfather's funeral. I was rather fond of my grandfather, even though the question always remained with me: 'Why did he have my brother out of school at weekends so many times without me?' Despite this we got along well. He often offered me words of wisdom, some of which stick with me. We were horse riding together one day and I had said something stupid, something flippant in order to make small talk. In his response, I feel he saw something in me that others hadn't. He said: "One day you will find yourself in a senior position and when you find yourself sitting at a table with people far better educated than yourself, remember it's bad enough for them to think you may be stupid, without you opening your mouth and confirming the fact. Always think before you speak and make what you say meaningful." I always try to remember this, especially in business.

I continued to travel the world. I travelled and I made business - Singapore, China, Canada, America, Russia, Australia, Israel, Africa, North and South America. And anywhere I wasn't able to make business I established contacts for future business. It all seemed to be going so well, that is until, in 2006 when I discovered IPS was being sold to another maritime company that wanted to break in to the world of tunnelling and I was being sold with it. One of the directors had suggested to the others if they were going to sell the tunnelling division they should discuss it with me. Not only would it have been courtesy to discuss it with me first but also many of the tunnel personnel considered themselves to be working for me rather than IPS - a maritime agency. The other directors ignored this advice and went ahead anyway, up to the point of shaking hands and opening the champagne, only to back out the following morning. The buyers – a Dutch company called Atlas Brunel - were furious, as was one of the IPS directors. I on the other hand was now feeling completely disrespected and decided to walk away. I resigned. IPS didn't want me to go and offered me a deal to stay that was very hard to turn down, however I knew they had been underpaying me on the original deal (remember the profit share issue) and was sure that it would be impossible for them to honour the new deal they were putting on the table. I called Claire and discussed it all with her; she said: "Great, come home." I called my closest friends and employees to tell them the situation. They told me they respected my actions and many said they would also now be resigning. They all told me they knew I would at some point set up my own company and I should let them know when I was ready as they would willingly join me. At the same time Atlas Brunel approached me and asked me to get involved in forming a new tunnelling company with them directly. While they were experts when it came to maritime personnel, they could see I had the expertise required to help them break in to supplying tunnelling personnel too. I went home, sat down with Claire and explained what the guys at Atlas Brunel were proposing. I told her what I thought I could do with them and the new company that was on the horizon. So much of my working life had already been spent away from home and I made it clear to Claire that if we embarked on this journey I would have to be all in. I didn't know how often I would be home and she'd be left 'holding the baby' - literally. She'd have to take care of the children, the home and everything on her own, as I would have to give my absolute everything to the new venture if it was to be a success. I knew it would pay off in the long run but if Claire had any doubts, I wasn't doing it. I explained if she agreed there would be no turning back but if she didn't like the idea, I'd take my chances back on the tools. I would only be building this new company if she was totally behind me. She assured me she backed me 100%.

Things then moved pretty damned quickly. We – the directors of Atlas Brunel and me - formed a company called International Tunnelling Services (ITS).

Back at home in Portishead I had now made a good circle of friends around me. I liked living in this coastal North Somerset town just a stone's throw away from the City of Bristol and close to good motorway links. I loved seeing my family settled there and enjoying life. Claire and I had had our eyes on a cottage in a lovely hamlet just outside Portishead, on the market for £330,000. It had land which would allow Claire to keep more horses. On the morning I was due to sign the contract for the formation of ITS, I mentioned to the directors we hadn't discussed goodwill. I was bringing a lot of tunnelling contacts and expertise to the business and I wanted something in return. I suggested £100,000 from each of the three directors. They weren't having any of it at first but I stood my ground and refused to sign the contract to form the business without it and so they eventually agreed. I could see those keys for the cottage, with mine and Claire's names on, just waiting for us!

Always one for pushing my luck, I now suggested that we also set up a maritime agency together. The new partners were rather reluctant as in their words: "You don't know anything about the maritime business." To which I replied: "That may be true but you know nothing about the tunnelling business." We formed a second business called International Crew Services (ICS) in 2007.

IPS had held me in such low regard that they hadn't placed a competition clause on me, so I was free to do as I wished, unrestricted. My secretary at IPS had been a very efficient Dutch lady called Simone. She had a great rapport with the field workers and I would have loved to have taken her with me to my new company but I didn't think she would get on with my other business partners. As a result, whilst businesswise it made sense to ask her to come with me, I knew it would be morally wrong. She was a single mother and I did not want to put her career in jeopardy. Unfortunately IPS didn't have the same scruples and dumped her soon after my departure.

Anja, a German administrator, did join me from IPS and we moved in to a rented office in Rotterdam, furnishing it with a plastic patio table and chairs. We had one laptop between us, using a dongle (stick) to access the internet and made ITS one side of the table and ICS the other. I set about travelling to jobsites making new contacts with potential clients, striking new contracts. I also took the opportunity to identify good personnel and invite them to come and work for me, including many employed by IPS. Being in demand, employees saw the opportunity to negotiate better salaries and as we had very few overheads, we were able to offer our workforce a good rate. Meanwhile, IPS however, desperate to hang on to their employees, decided to pay whatever it took to keep them. I had no intention of working for nothing and informed the men to make their choice with or without me.

40% stayed with IPS the others showed real loyalty and came with me to ITS.

For ICS I recruited the three best maritime personnel consultants from IPS, to develop the business. It grew very fast indeed. IPS paid a lot of money trying to stop me and my new Dutch partners. They hired a private detective to follow me and they even stole my phone number (which they then had to hand back), all to no avail.

As part of developing ITS I contacted Herrenknecht AG and they agreed to work directly with us for a special project in Bremen, North Germany. We supplied 24 specialist welders to work in arctic conditions. I visited the site and invited the dayshift team, who happened to be all Geordies, out for food and a couple of beers. It was a good evening and great for staff morale. On my next visit I took out the other team, who were all Scottish. Again we had a great night with good food and beer, but on this occasion it involved more and more beer, resulting in a very large bar bill! The next week my foreman called from the site informing me some of the men were complaining they had been paid short. My reply was to ask who they thought would pay for the gallons of beer and whisky they'd consumed on my last visit. Peter the foreman was shocked at this action but I explained after weighing the situation up, there was no way I was going to tell this team of half-drunk Scots they couldn't have any more beer on their night out. The project however, was yet another to add to our growing list of successfully completed contracts. Meanwhile, having put the right people in place to grow ICS, the company continued to go from strength to strength. By 2009 it had become a serious company within the maritime and offshore world and although I had a five year deal running with my partners from Atlas Brunel, they decided they wanted to buy me out early. We negotiated hard. One of the directors, Renee, was a fanatical football supporter of AZ, a Dutch football team and I had been invited a couple of times to watch them from the box he owned, centre field. At one game against Arsenal he somehow obtained the match ball signed by both teams and it now held prime place in his office. He and I were negotiating a million pound deal for my shares in ICS and I said I would only agree if he included the match ball. He flatly refused but I held the line and several hours later I drove away from his office with the ball and a deal on the table involving enough money to buy Goose Green! As for the future of the ball, I gave it to my son Kyle, telling him it was very special and he should look after it. I found it the next time I returned home, flat in the garden and the box was nowhere to be found.

Claire had mentioned to me that a house we knew well was for sale. It was adjacent to woodland, on a hill on the outskirts of Portishead and it had good energy. I took it upon myself to look in to it and decided it was ideal for us. Knowing funds from the ICS deal were imminent, I decided to buy it. I made an offer, which was accepted. There was just one problem, I hadn't yet got the money for it! I called my private banker Mike and told him I needed a million pound bridging loan. He went quiet, then told me Nat West couldn't do this but maybe Coutts & Co (the Queen's bank) could, if I could convince them I was worthy. I did and the deal was done.

I was still working out of the Netherlands office at this time but was now able to travel home more often. On one of my trips home, Claire and I loaded all our belongings in to cars and on to trailers and moved in to our new home, raising an eyebrow or two from the sellers who were still disposing of the contents of the property as we started moving in.

Following on from the success of the Bremen project the directors of Herrenknecht began to take a great deal of interest in me and in 2010 they asked me to attend an important meeting with them. It was arranged to take place at a hotel at Rotterdam Airport where they had flown in by private jet. They sat me down and asked me what my intentions were with ITS. I explained I had ambitions to provide services throughout the world and I had already started to do so. I also told them that if it proved successful enough, in the future I would consider becoming a contractor, taking on whole tunnelling projects, employing all the staff directly and overseeing it from beginning to end. They told me they'd been watching me closely for several years both in and out of work. They recognised that ITS was growing fast within the tunnelling industry and had a reputation for supplying good personnel. They didn't beat about the bush – they said they wanted 51% of ITS and asked how much this would cost. I still had the Dutch partners from Atlas Brunel involved with ITS which I feared might get in the way of a deal with Herrenknecht. There was a good offer on the table, better than good in fact, but I needed to work out what to do about the Atlas Brunel guys I was in business with. As I had done so before in the past, I manipulated the situation to my advantage and as part of the deal my Dutch partners were bought out by Herrenknecht and sent on their way.

CHAPTER 14

Small world

The deal with Herrenknecht was moving forward at pace. I hadn't even had time to discuss the 51% sale with Claire and the revenue of over a million pounds it would bring us but I knew she trusted me and always backed me.

With the other directors gone, it was now just me and Herrenknecht. When negotiating the 51% deal I had included in the agreement changing the name from International Tunnelling Services to Global Tunnelling Experts. It had also been agreed we would absorb Dan Tunnel, the Danish agency that had been supplying personnel to Herrenknecht. I think at this point Herrenknecht thought they would probably soon replace me with the guy heading up Dan Tunnel, but once they got their feet under the table they realised if they wanted to continue to grow globally, I was the person for the job. My strengths were and still are, without a doubt, travelling the world securing contracts, recruiting the right people for the job and looking after those people so that they look after us and the contract. Where I am not so strong – on the business admin side of things - I didn't need to worry. With Herrenknecht being a major company they were on top of everything from taxes to HR so I played to my strengths for the business while they played to theirs.

I was always aware of my physical and mental limits as I had been taken to them many times. I had worked out at an early stage that my limited education gave me a weakness so I worked extremely hard to catch up. Flying around the world on business trips, being in the air for long periods of time gave me ample time to read and learn, mostly from other people's mistakes as well as their successes. No-one can ever know everything, just as they can't be good at everything and so I knew if I was to be successful in business I needed support. I chose employees carefully, especially those who would complement my weaknesses. I have never been afraid of, or intimidated by, people who are smarter than me, in fact I see them as an asset and I am proud they allow me to lead and that includes my cleaner.

I was now committed to maximising my ability to develop Global Tunnelling Experts (GTE) into a truly global brand. As a 49% shareholder of GTE I travelled extensively, two and a half times around the world in fact, revisiting my contacts and making new ones, making business in nearly every country I visited.

On one particular business trip I found myself up-front in an Arab Emirates aeroplane flying first class from Dubai to Brisbane, Australia. I had never flown first class before and wouldn't have done then if it hadn't been so important for me to move quickly. Therefore I took the only seats available, which happened to be first class. Having taken off and levelled out, I realised I was alone with just a bar, three air hostess and a purser for company. We had plenty of time to chat and they asked where I was from. I told them I was from the Falkland Islands and they asked about the war. I told them about the two British Harriers we had seen bomb the Argentine airfield at Goose Green and that one of the British planes was shot down on the raid, the pilot killed. I also told them I was proud to have brought that pilot's uniform back to the UK and return it to his family, after finding it in the garage at Goose Green when looking for my motor bike. A bit later, when the plane's pilots changed over, I was approached by the captain of the plane. He said: "Mr Browning I have been sitting flying this plane wondering how to approach you." I immediately came back with: "You're not going to ask me to jump, right?" He replied: "No, but you told my crew about the raid at Goose Green in 1982, how you brought a pilot's uniform back to the UK and how happy the family were to receive it. Why did you do this?" I told him I didn't actually know but it just felt it was the right thing to do. He agreed and went on to tell me the name of the pilot. Surprised, I told him he was absolutely right about the name and asked how he knew it? He then looked me straight in the eyes and said: "Because I was the pilot of the other plane." We hugged, he cried, I thanked him and I realised just how small the world is. Sometimes you come across great leaders within companies. This is something I value as I don't think enough emphasis is placed on the importance of good leaders and managers. The pace of major projects is often down to the quality of the project managers, the decisions they make and the direction they give to their teams. Unfortunately I have come across plenty of bad leaders but I am pleased to say I have worked with many good ones too, some who are exceptional.

I had first met Philp in Singapore when he was working for Herrenknecht and valued his leadership skills and his ethics. After winning a contract in Belgium with Vinci I found Philip was now working for Vinci and I was delighted our paths had crossed once again. Philip was and still is a great leader; he is straight talking, is not afraid to make decisions and always gets the job done. I enjoy working with Philip and leaders like him; it's these kinds of people who stand out in the tunnelling world over the commercial managers who sometimes fail to offer direction to their teams.

GTE began setting up offices in countries we identified as tunnelling hotspots, some of them temporary, some of them permanent. With a number of tunnelling contracts coming our way and more on the cards, the UK was now one of those hotspots. Living in the West Country, it made perfect sense to set up an office in the South West and even more sense if it was in my neck of the woods. A new office block became available in Portishead and it seemed ideal. We signed the lease and set up our UK head office, right on my doorstep but just about far enough away from home for me to leave it behind at night if I chose to. I had, for some time, been employing tunnelling staff from in and around Portishead; identifying people with potential and offering them training to give them the chance of a good career ahead of them. Now I could do this in the admin field too. Over the coming years we built a team of loyal employees who, like our tunnelling teams in the field, learned if they worked hard and looked after us, we would in turn look after them.

I met Ash in around 2010. I hadn't realised at the time but we travelled on the Norland together in 1982, reminding me once again what a small world we live in. Ash had been a medic with 3 Para and had fought in the battle at Mt Longdon. He had sustained an injury which had put him on the Norland at the same time I was en route to the UK. Through my circle of friends in Portishead I had heard about this guy, who lived locally who'd served in the Falklands War. He had also heard about me. One sunny day, unbeknown to each other, we both just happened to be drinking in the garden at the Black Horse pub. We both stepped up to the outdoor serving hatch at the same time and our eyes locked. Having introduced ourselves we just clicked and it was the start of a good friendship. We discussed returning to the islands. Ash didn't feel ready. Eventually, however, we decided to make an informal trip back together. Once we arrived we travelled overland to Goose Green where I showed him the hall I'd been locked up in all those years ago and the spot where we had buried the dead Argentine soldiers. We then drove to Blue Beach to pay our respects at the British gravesides and then onto Green Beach where Ash had landed 35 years before. We stayed over with John and Michelle Jones, who now own the farm and some holiday lets. After some banter Ash asked John if he could have Green Beach. John said as he had 1600 acres he couldn't see why not, as long as Ash returned each year to maintain ownership, making sure the beach was kept in good order. Nothing came of that and so John has now given the beach to me!

In 1982 3 Para had tabbed 61 miles to Estancia House in preparation to retake Mt Longdon. We visited Estancia House and as we approached Ash confessed the last time he had been there, after a briefing in the house, he had stolen some lamb and rice to add to the military compo rations they had been living on for the two weeks since landing at Green Beach. I told him I knew the people, a lovely couple called Ailsa and Tony, who lived in the house. Ash wanted to own up and settle his debt so I introduced him and explained the situation. Looking at Ash, Ailsa said: "What did you take chey?" (Chey is a term of endearment used by Kelpers as we would use the word mate in the UK) Ash told her and took his wallet from his pocket (which doesn't happen very often!) and asked: "How much do I owe you?" Ailsa looked him directly in the eye, shook her head and said: "No son, how much do we owe you?" This sums up the gratitude we (those from the Falklands) feel towards those who liberated us from the invading forces in 1982.

Back in the UK, Ash had been contemplating leaving his job with the fire service and so I talked to him about working for me as a consultant on the recruitment side of things at GTE. We shook hands on it and he came to work for me, but not before agreeing, no matter what happened in work, we would always remain friends.

In 2014 I travelled to Istanbul, Turkey. I had been contacted by the Turkish company Yapi, which was responsible for building a tunnel under the Bosporus Strait, a waterway which splits Asia and Europe. They needed the expertise of GTE and asked me to go out to meet with them. I invited Ash, as one of my consultants, to come with me. The meeting room was very large and we sat down with the whole Yapi management team. After going through the normal formalities we were about to discuss their needs when the door opened and a very smartly dressed gentleman entered. The room fell silent and as I was sitting closest to the door I stood up and shook his hand introducing myself as the managing director of GTE. The room erupted with laughter and when things eventually settled down someone explained this was the tea boy I had just greeted. I complimented him on his smart appearance and asked how long had he been working for Yapi. No-one seemed to know. I asked the Yapi team when his birthday was, they didn't know that either. I suggested he was a very important member of the team and told them in my company I make it my business to know when everyone's birthday is, including my cleaner and if I could afford a tea boy, I would for sure know when his birthday was. At the end of the meeting Yapi agreed to work with me and I reckon they also found out when their tea boy's birthday was for the future!

CHAPTER 15

GTE Doha

In 2015 Herrenknecht successfully sold 21 tunnel boring machines to Qatar for a complete metro system - 56 kilometres of tunnels - a huge infrastructure undertaking and like an awful lot of projects I have come across, they had forgotten the main ingredient to make it all come together - skilled personnel. I had anticipated this and was ready and waiting. I met with Sheikh Mohammed, an important contact for this business contract. I did my research prior to meeting him, as I always do when meeting a potential client. I discovered he was very interested in history and has written books on the history of Qatar, so I took him a map of the Falkland Islands that shows the known ship wrecks around the islands (before the Panama Canal ships had to sail past the Falklands en route to Cape Horn and many didn't make it due to the severity of the Atlantic Ocean conditions). The map of the Falkland Islands now hangs on his office wall.

We set up a full subsidiary in Doha to facilitate the requirements, with me often working from Sheikh Mohammed's office. The Doha contract was a hugely import one and I needed someone based in Doha to oversee the day to day running of the business in Qatar. Ash told me about a guy called Paul who lived in Clevedon, the next town to Portishead, where Ash had grown up and where I now lived. Paul had a good business background but was now semi-retired, he didn't need to work for the money but apparently remained driven and is always interested in a challenge. I arranged to meet Paul on the course at Clevedon Golf Club and after a good chat knew he was more than capable of managing GTE's operations in Doha. We agreed that sometime in the future he would at least visit the set up in Doha. That meeting was on the Friday and the following Tuesday I gave him a call and asked if he was busy on Thursday. He said he was available and asked why, so I explained he was booked on a flight to Doha with me and sent him the flight details. Once there, he agreed to manage GTE Doha for me and he stayed there doing a fine job for two-and-a-half years. He's still employed by GTE today and is a very well respected commercial manager within the company.

The Doha project was a complete success, largely due to the support of the skilled personnel supplied by GTE and the professionalism shown by the workforce despite extreme temperatures, often above 50 degrees. And the management of course! We had key personnel on all twenty-one TBMs, as well as the complete workforce needed for the 60 kilometres of conveyor systems used to transport the material that was bored from the ground to make room for the metro. The project even made the book of Guinness World Records for the most TBMs running concurrently on one project.

GTE gets little or no outside recognition for the support we give to so many major infrastructure projects around the world, but those within the industry know how much we do and that's what matters to me.

While the Doha project was in progress I had gone to an oil expo in Brazil and while there I received a random call from someone claiming to be from the Miami office of the World Bank. They explained they had a client in the Dominican Republic that had acquired a TBM to use in the building of their metro network and asked if I was able to go out and check the TBM before they started their operations. I flew out to Miami to meet the person I had been talking to before flying over to the Dominican Republic to meet their client. It turned out that a close relative of the president had acquired a TBM but it was and had been sitting for some time on the docks, uncovered and exposed to the elements. I called Oliver, who was head of field services at Herrenknecht and he joined me in the Dominican Republic with a team to put together a report for the client. His inspection confirmed that a huge amount of money would need to be spent before this TBM could be used to build anything, let alone a metro.

We were able to help and with the right specialists provided, the TBM was soon extending the Dominican Republic's metro.

CHAPTER 16

Everyone deserves a chance

I have always tried to be fair and ethical and I believe in treating people how you would like to be treated yourself.
Have I been lucky? Yes I think I have, but I also believe that to a certain degree you make your own luck in this world. I was lucky Tommy Snr gave me a chance to get in to tunnelling all those years ago, but I made the best of that luck and worked hard, firstly to show my appreciation to him and secondly to reap the rewards of that hard work. I feel everyone should be given opportunities in life, whether they take them and make the most of them is up to them, but everyone deserves a chance. I have tried to ensure I provide opportunities for people throughout my working life and I will always try to do this. I have learned much by reading stuff over the years, I have also learned a great deal

by trial and error, going with my gut instincts, listening to people and negotiating with them. I have learned a great deal from leaders that have led me too. I have learned from the good ones and from the bad ones I have learned how not to lead and manage a team. I have also learned the importance of family support for those, including me, who work away from home. I can't highlight enough how extremely important that support from family is.

For many years I made it my mission to seek the best training facilities for our workforce, so they could learn hands-on from some of the best. This has involved familiarising skilled people with the latest developments and up-skilling the semi-skilled. I approached the owner of Herrenknecht, Dr Martin Herrenknecht, directly and was able to convince him to allow GTE to send personnel to his huge facilities in Germany where the finest TBMs were made. I knew that to see the workings firsthand would give the workers so much more understanding. Some of the managers within the factory were opposed to the idea; I think they felt threatened by a sudden influx of 'outsiders' taking an interest in their work. I guessed there would be some hostility towards the first workers to go in so I began by sending in my own son, Kyle. I suspected he wouldn't get an easy ride and he didn't, but I knew he was capable of dealing with it. He did a good job and as others followed, slowly but surely they were accepted, even if for some it was through gritted teeth. The training paid dividends and not only helped the workforce improve their skills and understanding, but for many it also fired a passion for this massive and powerful equipment that could do such great work.

That wasn't the only time Kyle came across hostility in his work, being the son of the boss wasn't easy. It became even more difficult when I sent him to Argentina to work on a TBM and the project engineer thought it comical to inform the Argentine workforce that Kyle's father was from the Falkland Islands and had fought the Argentines in the war.

Kyle worked hard to overcome the hostilities by showing he can work as hard as the best of them and it has paid off with him now being a respected senior within the company.

I like to think I'm a good judge of character. I might not get it right every time but nine times out of 10, I reckon I do. GTE has plenty of success stories, far too many for me to mention in this book but I've chosen a few to highlight.

I seem to meet a lot of good people at my local watering hole. I met Andy a few years ago. Andy's a people's person and a real good egg. We got on well and despite him being old enough and wealthy enough to retire, he agreed to join the GTE team and works on the recruitment and personnel side of things. He says he enjoys coming to work and for that I am thankful.

A good friend of mine, Richard, owns a garage which he runs with his sons. He's one of the best mechanical engineers I know. Richard always says you should try and learn something new every day. Words of wisdom that I use often when speaking to young people who work for me at GTE, including two of Richard's sons! Claire one day told me about a young buck called Jack. Jack hadn't had the best start in life and had found it difficult after being bounced around a variety of foster homes during his childhood. He hadn't been able to find work and was feeling pretty fed up. I had planned some heavy work at our stables over the weekend and suggested Claire asked him to come and help me at 8am on Saturday morning. I arrived at 7.30am and Jack was already there waiting; that was a good start in my book. You can tell a good worker quick enough if you've worked hard yourself. Jack impressed me sufficiently for me to offer him a trainee position at GTE. He has since up-skilled at every opportunity and is a valuable asset to the team.

Before we set up the UK head office in Portishead, when I was home I used to work out of a small office which overlooked Portishead High Street. I would regularly look out of the window and see a small crowd of lads who had left school and not found work. They tended to gather at the entrance to an alleyway and smoke something that smelled a bit funny, which definitely wasn't tobacco. They weren't going to find work doing that every day I thought, as they caught my eye from my window. As I watched, for me one of them stood out from the crowd. One day as the others left, I pulled this chap aside and had a word in his ear suggesting he could really make something of himself if he gave up the funny stuff and concentrated on finding a career. Some weeks later he knocked the office door brandishing a certificate from the doctor confirming he had no illegal substances in his bloodstream. I gave him a start. He trained, he learned and he progressed. He has worked well for GTE and has saved himself a very healthy deposit for a house that he is in the process of buying with his partner. Once again, this demonstrates some people just need to be given a chance.

I took great delight (and still do) in recruiting young people, and not so young people, who don't have academic qualifications on paper but who have demonstrated skill, determination and ability with practical, hands-on work and successfully putting them through training with GTE. Many of them excelled after doing training at factories and on-site in different parts of the world, but I was keen to open our own training centre, preferably on home turf. We opened the GTE Training Academy alongside the GTE UK office in Portishead in January 2022 and whilst we will use it to train our workers, I am also keen to see the training centre utilised by the wider business community for industry and commerce. We now run training courses ranging from first aid and mental health awareness courses through to CITB on-site health and safety and specialist training for the construction and tunnelling industry. We are also giving free use of the centre to first aid training sessions for children. If it helps save just one life it will have been well worth it.

I get a huge amount of satisfaction knowing that by creating GTE and supplying workforces to tunnelling projects around the globe, me and my teams at GTE have helped thousands of families pay their bills, put food on the table and even enjoy holidays and life's little luxuries. My entrepreneurial spirit has resulted in millions of pounds going in to the UK's coffers too.

One thing I am sure about is that without the skills, professionalism and dedication of our loyal teams, there would be no GTE. I am proud of everyone who has worked or is working with me and for me.

CHAPTER 17

Pushing for change

In 2021 I was asked to join The Leaders Council of Great Britain and through this organisation I have made it my mission to call for change.

The Leaders Council describes itself as an organisation "for the people who run the country and the people who keep the country running". Chaired by former Home Secretary and Education Secretary, Lord Blunkett, The Leaders Council celebrates the hard work and achievements of the nation's unsung leaders, while laying the ground for the next generation. Through detailed case studies, news coverage, podcasts and leadership events, the organisation aims to present the authentic voice of British industry.

With GTE working in 48 different countries, supporting around 145 major infrastructure projects using skilled personnel of approximately 37 different nationalities, I feel a worthy member. Through The Leaders Council I have called for scrupulous operations among businesses in the UK and a government crackdown on companies who flout rules and regulations, especially around tax and national insurance payments. It has always been important to me that GTE operates with integrity at all times but I do feel it sometimes puts us at a disadvantage over others that have a less stringent approach. I am also, through the Leaders Council, pushing for government reform when it comes to education and academic qualifications. I am calling for them to place more importance, than there currently is, on hands-on experience. Having seen so many young people who thought there were little career prospects for them, having failed their GCSEs, join GTE's training programme and go on to carve a very successful career for themselves, I am keen to back apprenticeships and on-site training. However, I am also urging Westminster to consider, for experienced personnel, introducing accreditation through proven past work. I am a believer that, rather than accreditation having to be earned from scratch, we can get skilled and semi-skilled people into work and progress their careers by means of accreditation through proven past experience, done through certified CVs and references. When trying to further their career many people are being excluded from the selection process because they do not have the correct qualifications on paper, even though based on their experience, they may be able to do the job standing on their head! Issuing qualifications based on past experience and achievements could help overcome this, thus opening up job opportunities to those who have proved themselves in a role even though they don't have the correct GCSE or NVQ certificates.

Through the Leaders Council I will continue to push for changes I believe will help the UK industry reduce the gap in its skills shortage.

I am, to a certain extent, influenced by my study of Genghis Khan. He had a poor childhood and rough upbringing but despite his hardships he went on to be a mighty warrior and leader. He proved to be a good judge of character, promoting his officers and recognising leaders based on experience and delivery of skills, regardless of their race, religion, beliefs and background. He rewarded loyalty and good work and more importantly he held people to account for their actions. All these are things for which I have great respect.

In addition to backing apprenticeships and training and calling for accreditation through experience, I will also continue to encourage organisations to invest more in leadership skills. So many companies spend hundreds of thousands of pounds training staff, only to put them on a project to find they have little or no direction because the leaders are failing. This is definitely something I would like to see improved in industry.

The Royal Military Academy Sandhurst (RMAS) is where all officers in the British Army are trained to take on the responsibility of leading their soldiers.

Sandhurst is recognised as a world-leading military training academy and delivers a variety of leadership development training courses to a wide number of countries across the globe. During training, all officer cadets learn to live by the academy's motto: 'Serve to Lead'. Even after leaving Sandhurst young officers are carefully guided by corporals and sergeants who have the hands-on experience of reality to benefit those they are guiding in to the world of leadership. Unfortunately in many industries, including the construction world, we have engineers who become leaders without the training and guidance from those with extensive experience to help them become good leaders. Instead they are often influenced by commercial teams, who so often have their own agenda. It is important that we correct this and recognise the importance of promoting good leadership skills.

It's worth remembering... wrong decisions in peace time cost millions of pounds, wrong decisions in war time costs lives and millions of pounds.

CHAPTER 18

Proud

I know that in building a successful career, which has benefitted my family, friends, workforce and in fact people around the world, there has been a price to pay; sacrifices have been made. I'm thinking back now to Johnny Cash's song, Cat's In The Cradle.

Yes I have missed out on some things in life but I have also had some amazing experiences that as a child and young man I never thought possible. I am extremely proud of what I have achieved and I am extremely proud of my family.

I have been completely open about my love for Claire, she really is the love of my life, my soul mate and so why, you may be thinking, does she not feature more in this book? Well let me tell you, Claire is a very private person. She is very confident in her own world and chooses not to venture in to fields she is uncomfortable with and I respect this. She is kind, loving, sexy and beautiful. She is a great wife, mother, grandmother, daughter, sister, friend and companion. She is led by her spirit and her conscience. She supports me in everything I do, but she chooses not to be directly involved in my work and that works for us. She did a grand job bringing up our three boys, often singlehandedly while I was away working, and she is doing a lot of good with her equine and nature therapy centre. I am so very proud of her but she prefers me not to shout about it.

As for my children...

Shane

I tried hard to keep in touch with Shane, my eldest son, and for the most part we managed to keep a relationship going. After trying his hand at a few things in the UK, Shane decided to make a new life for himself in the Falklands. I am proud to say he is now a policeman in the Falklands living with his beautiful Scottish wife, Bex and my granddaughter. His wedding in

Scotland was a fantastic family affair and I am so pleased to report we keep in touch regularly now.

Stacie

Maintaining contact and any kind of relationship with my second eldest child and only daughter, Stacie, proved more difficult, which saddens me no end. I have connected with her a couple of times now, especially at Shane's wedding and I live in hope that one day we will be able to make our peace. She has a strong spirit and I have no doubt she will do well in whatever she chooses to do.

Kyle

Kyle, my eldest son with Claire, having served seven years in the field as a mechanical engineer throughout the world for Herrenknecht AG and GTE, is now a senior consultant for the growing company (GTE). He has shown great promise and I have sometimes put him in difficult situations, but he has always handled them with professionalism and is definitely a chip off the old block! Kyle has a son with his fiancée Aimee (who works in the GTE office) and they are building a good future together.

Jack

Jack tried construction but it didn't float his boat, he probably needs something with more soul. He has mastered playing the guitar and enjoys making music. He has passed his driving test and has his independence which I am sure will help him with his aspirations to travel, to explore the depths of lesser know territories and experience different cultures. Jack is funny too. He'll make a brilliant stand-up comedian one day and has written lots of his own material. He was due to take a spot at a well known comedy club but the pandemic closed it down before he got a chance to shine. Jack's a deep thinker. Reflecting, he once told me: "Pa, the trouble with you and the older generation is that you have too much in your head. It's easier to just use Google!"

Flynn

While Flynn didn't show an interest in the tunnelling industry or construction, he is definitely showing some of my entrepreneurial spirit. Having trained as a barber, he is now happy running his own successful barbershop business just a few miles from the family home. Flynn is also a social animal with a good crowd of friends. I am extremely proud of all five of my children. They are doing very well for themselves despite not attending private schools. They have not been spoilt, they have not had a privileged upbringing, they have all had to work hard to get where they are today and I hope, in fact I feel confident, they will all continue to work hard to make their way in life and will all be successful in their own way, no matter what path they choose. All I ask is they are happy, healthy and kind.

CHAPTER 19

Support

Being successful in business has allowed me to give back financially as well as in other ways.

I have on occasion invested in the business ideas of local entrepreneurs and sometimes former employees of GTE. However, I recognise I do not have the time or manpower to carry out due diligence or monitor operations for other businesses. I have lost thousands of pounds investing in businesses outside my control, which have subsequently not been successful. I have learned lessons from this and have since made a pact with myself not to invest in any businesses I am unable to personally control. My experiences make it easier for me to now understand the BBC TV programme, Dragon's Den!

I am, however, happy to financially help good causes.

Over the next few pages I am pleased to introduce just a few of the charities that are very close to my heart, which I am pleased to be able to support.

Cockleshell Endeavour

Run by former Royal Marine Commando, Mick Dawson, the Cockleshell Endeavour is a project that supports veterans through water based adventures. It is a resource to help recovering veterans back onto the path to recovery. The organisation uses expeditions, races and adventures as a tool to plan a way forward through whatever challenges veterans may face, be it physical or mental health.

I was introduced to Mick by Marty, who I met at a Remembrance Parade in Bath. Marty was one of the Royal Marines honoured to have been selected by 2 Para to accompany them on the liberation of Goose Green back in 1982. He told me about Mick and suggested I might like to meet him and so it was arranged.

I liked Mick and I liked what he was doing with Cockleshell Endeavour, so it was agreed I would offer his project some sponsorship.

Mick is a filmmaker, professional sailor, adventurer and author, my favourite of his books being 'Never Leave A Man Behind'. He is perhaps best known for rowing the Pacific Ocean with friend and fellow ocean rower Chris Martin in a new state of the art vessel, Bojangles, which Mick built. In 2018, Mick successfully rowed the Pacific with fellow veteran Steve Sparkes who, in doing so, became the first blind person ever to do that.

To mark 40 years since the Falklands War, Mick and Steve, better known as Sparky, embarked on a paddle, in a two man kayak, from the Commando Memorial at Spean Bridge, Scotland, to the Yomper statue in Southsea. They started on 2nd April 2022, finishing on 14th June, with their journey taking the exact duration of the 1982 Falklands War. Throughout their journey they were joined by fellow Falklands veterans and anyone else who had connections to the conflict all those

years ago. They stopped off at towns and cities en route recording stories and firsthand accounts from all they met who were affected by the war in any way. These stories will be added to Mick's growing archives of the Falklands War. Cockleshell Endeavour raises money for the Royal Marines Charity.
www.cockleshellendeavour.com

The Parachute Regimental Association
The Parachute Regimental Association (PRA) was formed at the end of the Second World War to further the interests of The Parachute Regiment and to organise functions and activities so members could continue associations formed during their service with the Regiment and Airborne Forces.

PRA membership covers all age groups and different cap badges with branches nationwide, including Northern Ireland. Meetings are generally held monthly to organise social functions, visits, reunions, pilgrimages, battlefield tours and, of course, to catch up on the latest

Regimental news and gossip over a drink or two.

The PRA, in partnership with other Regimental Charities, provides welfare support and advice to those in need or distress. The PRA's objectives are to promote the efficiency of The Parachute Regiment and Airborne Forces by fostering esprit de corps and maintaining contact between past and present members. They offer support to those serving or who have served in The Parachute Regiment and Airborne Forces, or their dependants. This association is also involved in the commemoration and remembrance of members of The Parachute Regiment and Airborne Forces who have died while on active service and the encouragement of public recognition of the sacrifice made by such people.

The Airborne Forces Security Fund (AFSF) and the Parachute Regiment Charity (PRC) have now merged to form The Parachute Regiment and Airborne Forces Charity (PRAFC).

www.theparachuteregimentalassociation.com

Elm Tree Farm Wellbeing Centre

It is my pleasure to not only invest financially in Claire's equine and nature therapy facility, but also invest time to physically support it on site.

The centre, based on our land, offers green open space providing opportunities for children and young people to connect with nature to benefit their mental wellbeing. The centre supports those who experience, or have experienced, social and emotional trauma and those who may have reduced attention and concentration spans. The equine assisted learning at Elm Tree Farm Wellbeing Centre provides a unique learning experience using horses as active participants. The natural responses of the horses give those working with them a deeper understanding of themselves. The centre also has small animals for petting and observing and gardening provision as well as woodland and nature therapy to help reduce anxiety, stress and anger. Its activities promote emotional awareness, empathy, trust and relationship building; help elevate self-esteem, assist in the development and

improvement of social skills and problem-solving skills, boost confidence, build resilience and help establish boundaries. The work is aimed at providing therapeutic interventions to help improve how the children and young people attending feel, think and behave, which in turn can also support better learning in school, college or in a workplace.
www.elmtreewellbeing.co.uk

CHAPTER 20

Reflection

As I look back on my life I am fiercely proud of all I have achieved, it could so easily have all gone very wrong for me, but largely, I chose the positive. I am now not many years away from turning 60 but there is still so much I want to do. I am asked if I have thought about retirement and the honest truth is - it has reared its head in my mind once or twice. I have however immediately shut the thought down when I think of all the teams working hard around the world making a difference to the infrastructure in so many different lands and what is still left to do. I look at Dr Martin Herrenknecht who still has drive and integrity as he turns 80-years-old and I look at the workforces who depend on their role within GTE to provide for themselves and their families.

No-one is indispensable and I know the world of tunnelling will still turn without Kevin Browning, but Kevin Browning enjoys securing new business, Kevin Browning enjoys looking after his workforce and Kevin Browning still gets a buzz when he sees the successful completion of a huge project he has secured the contract for and overseen. So I ask myself the question: "Why on earth would Kevin Browning want to retire?"

At the moment I continue to get a great deal of satisfaction from my work but am also lucky enough to be able to choose to take time out when I want to. I reckon I've got the best of both worlds and I'm loving it!

On returning to the Falklands from time to time it never fails to amaze me how robust and positive the people living there remain. The islands are without doubt one of, if not the most, patriotic places in the world. Of course there is now a telephone network and TV. They also have regular supply ships and planes flying to deliver goods. If you need something that's not on the island, you might not get it the next day but you're likely to be able to obtain it within a few days, very different to when I lived there.

Some people, on and from the islands, have fared better than others for sure, but they wouldn't have been able to achieve what they have without the support and commitment of others and I sincerely hope they remember this as they climb the ladder of success.

It pleases me a great deal to see the younger generation from the Falkland Islands rising up through the ranks of authority and getting involved with the decision making that will affect the lives of those who live on the islands and of future generations.

Some residents of the Falklands say I walked out on them, turned my back and left them, but whilst I did walk away, I don't see quite it like they do. I didn't intentionally desert them, I just had a strong desire to give something back and I didn't feel I could do that if I remained on the islands. I hope through my actions people now feel that I have given something back, from family members on the islands who I have supported and my military service for the land that liberated us, through to business dealings around the world that have provided opportunities for others.

The fact remains that none of this would have been possible, for me or those making lives for themselves in the modern-day Falkland Islands, had the soldiers, sailors, airmen and civilians who fought and died in order to liberate us in 1982, not done so. For that, from the bottom of my heart, I say thank you.

FOR YOUR INFORMATION

GLOBAL TUNNELLING EXPERTS

Global Tunnelling Experts (GTE) continues to provide skilled personnel to the tunnelling industry worldwide. In a volatile world that requires agile management, GTE is a partner for all human resource solutions. It is an experienced provider of qualified workforce for all jobs throughout all construction phases on tunnel construction sites and beyond. Having a skilled workforce supporting any project is key to its success. GTE helps organisations to choose the right experts. It can provide a whole site crew or find the right specialist to perfectly complement a team, whether in the short or long term. GTE offers an all-around service and advice for all phases, finding the ideal recruitment solutions for any project. It guarantees quality - anywhere, any time!

www.global-tunnelling-experts.com

GTE TRAINING ACADEMY

GTE Training Academy is a CITB and City and Guilds fully accredited training provider offering quality specialist training for the tunnelling and construction industries. Its centre, based in Portishead near Bristol, is just a five minute drive from junction 19 of the M5 motorway, 10 miles from the City of Bristol and its main rail links and less than a 30 minute drive from Bristol International Airport.

It offers training within the centre which boasts state of the art facilities and equipment and can also offer virtual training and on-site training.

In addition the centre offers first aid accredited training for all types of businesses and organisations.

www.gteta.com

Acknowledgements

There are many, many people I would like to thank for being a part of my life's journey, which in turn has enabled me to write my story and create No Ordinary Man. I would need another book if I were to list everyone! To all those who have helped me on my way, for better or worse, I thank you.

Special thanks go to my family for understanding, supporting and putting up with me while I wrote this book. I would also like to thank everyone who has assisted me during my adventures that helped me achieve success, including the people who have underestimated me; it's all added to my winding, colourful path. And finally, thank you to my editor Tracey Fowler, for agreeing to work with me, for being by my side as we travelled through my past and then for making my notes, which at times could be random, in to readable sense.

Editor's note

Whilst I accept it is somewhat unusual, it has become customary for me when working as an editor on autobiographies, to add an editor's note. This is because I always feel extremely privileged to have been allowed in to the fold of the writer's circle, to share so many corners of their life and as a result play an important part in the creation of their book. For me it is an honour to be involved in this way.

For many months I have probed the ins and outs of Kevin's life, both personal and business, for which I feel there is only a very fine line between.

I hope readers will find interest in Kev's adventures, feel inspired by his achievements and embrace opportunities with confidence as a result of reading his story.

Kevin Browning, thanks for inviting me along for the ride. The journey has been an interesting one and one I have thoroughly enjoyed every minute of. Long may you continue to make a difference.

T x

Printed in Great Britain
by Amazon

84718500R00108